# On This Rock I Stand

# On This Rock I Stand

## And Other Messages

**Vance Havner**

**BAKER BOOK HOUSE**
Grand Rapids, Michigan 49506

Formerly published under
the title, *Vance Havner: Just a Preacher*

**Library of Congress Cataloging in Publication Data**

Havner, Vance, 1901-
    Vance Havner, just a preacher.

    1. Baptists — Sermons.    2. Sermons, American.
I. Title.
BX6333.H345V36          252'.3          81-11195
ISBN: 0-8010-4296-8          AACR2

# Contents

# Foreword

'Not since Manhattan Island was sold for $24.00 has there been so much dirt available for so little money as now."

Vance Havner, in his own unique way, has traveled the length and breadth of America, calling our nation to repentance and faith. At the age of twelve he began to preach in the hill country of North Carolina and has preached well over 13,000 sermons since then.

The heart of his ministry is revival. Courageously he speaks to our age, convicting our hearts, revealing our sins, and pointing to Jesus Christ as the only remedy. Havner says, "The tragedy of the hour is that the situation is desperate, but the saints are not. If they were, we would have revival."

I first heard Vance Havner as a boy in our home church. It was his gift of humor that captured me in those early days. He rebuked us, but in a palatable way. Vance Havner has the ability to say tough things tenderly and even humorously.

He has preached at conferences at Moody Bible Institute for forty years. Thousands of students and Christian workers have been revived and recharged through his ministry. He is a favorite among the students and pastors, even at eighty years of age.

Billy Graham says of Vance Havner, "I do not know of any man in my generation who has so stirred revival fires in hearts of so many people throughout the nation as has Vance Havner. Great crowds of people have packed churches and auditoriums to hear him preach . . . . Whenever I see a book by Vance Havner I immediately purchase it, because I know that I am going to get some good thoughts for my own sermon material. I, along with thousands of clergy from all denominations throughout the country, owe a great debt of gratitude to Vance Havner. . . . Always, on every occasion he has given the glory to the Lord Jesus Christ."*

I trust that this book, made up of what we think is the best of Vance Havner's writings, will be a challenge and blessing to you.

GEORGE SWEETING
President, Moody Bible Institute

*From *Vance Havner: Journey from Jugtown* by Douglas M. White, copyright 1977 by Douglas M. White, published by Fleming H. Revell Company. Used by permission.

# Interview with Vance Havner

*Not long before Vance Havner's eightieth birthday, author Jerry Jenkins visited with him at his home in Greensboro, North Carolina. Following are excerpts from that conversation.*

**VH:** My wife passed away seven years ago, when I was seventy-three. That was a turning point in my life, of course. I wrote the little book *Though I Walk Through the Valley,* and I have heard more from it than I have from all the others.

**JJ:** Because it hit people where they lived?

**VH:** I didn't try to explain it. Nobody can. I just wrote the way I felt. And, friend, not many days go by that I don't hear from people in sorrow, bereaving, in trouble. I didn't realize what some people are going through until I wrote that book. You don't know how to comfort people if you haven't been down their road. They like to know what you know about it.

These last seven years have been my most fruitful, I think. I never dreamed at this age I would be going like I am. It's too much, but I haven't got my wife to hold me back now, and I like to be busy. I come to this apartment, open the door, and nobody is here to meet me. In motels nobody meets me but a blank wall. And that's not a picnic, brother, when it's nearly every day in the year. Every week you're readjusting to a new bed, and a new everything. I've seen preachers try it a year or two and say, "Man, I've got to get back to my bed." Only by the grace of God, I've made it.

9

JJ: People who don't do your type of work think it sounds glamorous.

VH: How wonderful. Live in motels, and travel.

JJ: It wears thin pretty fast, doesn't it?

VH: Billy Graham said the other day—and he is just sixty-two—"Thirty years of hotel life are beginning to work on me." I thought, *Brother, wait until you're eighty, and then you've had fifty years of it.* I've been sixty-seven years in the ministry.

JJ: A lot of things have changed in sixty-seven years.

VH: Sure. When you fly today, you're looking down on an ocean and clouds maybe, whereas in the old days you went through the country and saw how people lived. What is worth going 600 miles an hour to get to? You can't think slow and ride fast somehow. You know I ride first class. I have to pet myself a little in these latter years. I'm not going to sit back there on all the long trips jammed in there. The other day I took a short flight, tourist, and a great big fat woman, who needed three seats, came and plugged herself in, and I nearly died in there.

JJ: You used to travel everywhere with your wife?

VH: I was married in 'forty and Sarah traveled with me for thirty-three years. Back in 'thirty-eight I was still in Charleston, the First Baptist Church. But I was beginning to travel and preach in the summer, and I came down with two years of nervous exhaustion and insomnia and depression. I wouldn't wish it on a dog. And I didn't know what in the world to do. I didn't want to talk to anybody about it. You couldn't talk to preachers about things like that.

JJ: How did it manifest itself?

VH: I went to bed one night and I mean, I didn't sleep. Same thing the next night and the next night. I catnapped along the way, or I'd have been dead. Yet the Lord was opening these doors. I said, "Lord, I can't sleep in any bed, let alone a different one every week. I can't do this." But finally I resigned my pastorate and started out. The first date I had was at Mel Trotter's Mission in Chicago, but I never even got to it. I came down with the flu in Chicago, and they put me in the hospital.

I lay there, and the devil sat at the foot of the bed and said, "Now, what are you going to do? You can't preach, and you gave up your church." But Sarah was willing to undertake life with me in my condition. We took off with not much money, and me half sick. Yet we never lacked friends, never lacked for calls, never lacked for anything. I never realized what I had until I didn't have her. I thought I did. It was hard, but we had such a wonderful time.

I recently found a handful of old love letters I'd written to her, just before we got married. She didn't know it then, but I was not only trying to persuade her, I was trying to persuade myself. Now I can see how the hand of God was in the whole business. I said let's make the venture. The letters were in the old house she grew up in. I found them in an old trunk. Just looked like they were saved for this day for me.

JJ: How were things with your wife say in nineteen seventy-one, 'seventy-two just before she died?

VH: Things had opened up so much for us. We made a trip to Europe and Israel, and we had gotten a new apartment. We bought us a car. We were really enjoying going here and yonder. But then Sarah took sick all summer and into the fall.

JJ: So it wasn't a real prolonged thing?

VH: No. But she had so many ailments. Satan tried to discourage me and put me in a state myself, asking why, why, why? Well, humanly I *did* ask why. But if the devil was trying to overthrow my faith, he missed the mark, because I came out stronger.

JJ: What did it do to your ministry at that time? You must have had to curtail some of your traveling.

VH: Yes. And yet the doctor told me, "Don't stay here in this hospital so much. Get out and go preach. We're taking care of her." One of my books, *Hope Thou in God,* is a result of that. I was up to Hickory for a meeting. I walked into the motel, low as I could be. My mind and heart were with Sarah. A Gideon Bible was lying open to the only place in it where three times on the same two pages you have the same verse. "Why art thou cast down, O my soul? and why art thou disquieted within me? hope thou in God . . . I shall yet praise Him." Well, some folks would call that coincidence. But I wouldn't, not this time. This was providence, not coincidence. Once in a while the Lord arranges things.

JJ: Where were you when your wife died?

VH: I was with her. She died at two fifteen Sunday morning, and I preached at eleven.

JJ: That sermon is the first in this book. Was it difficult to preach that morning?

VH: No, it wasn't. It's a strange thing. The impact of it doesn't come for the first day. But as we rode out to the cemetery and the door of the hearse was half open—I don't know why—but I could see the casket inside. And the little word *gone* came over me. And I wrote a whole chapter, "She is gone." But I haven't lost her, because I know where she is.

JJ: Did you go through real dark times then after it sank in?

VH: Yes, loneliness. Human, you know. I cried like nobody's business. And that's human. And you better cry. Because God put those ducts in there for some purpose.

JJ: The rest of the sermons in this book are from your

Moody Bible Institute Founder's Week messages over the years.

VH: I've been to Moody so much. I've been fifteen times to Founder's Week, every other year or so.

I marvel at that place every time I go up there. Those great buildings. And if we had been going over the country with a fine-toothed comb looking for the next great evangelist, D. L. Moody would have been the last prospect. He didn't look it or anything. There is only one way to explain that man. That's to say, it's God. The work of God.

Moody had been dead since before I was born, yet God has put the right people there to continue the basic traditions. There must have been an awful lot of prayer behind that place, because it's weathered all these years. I had a good time up there last time. I spoke on not missing your miracle. Several fellows in the Bible missed theirs: the rich young ruler, the old disobedient prophet, and king Saul. God's got something, I said, for you. My father was called to preach, but he never preached. When I started out as a kid, he was so happy. But I couldn't live his life, and he couldn't live mine.

JJ: You had a rough spell there, didn't you?

VH: Yeah, later. There's almost an unavoidable teenage and later crisis. It comes to everybody. I wasn't too well grounded in doctrine those days.

JJ: You know, so many people who became Christians as children go through some sort of a second encounter with God. It's simply, finally, saying, Hey, is this going to be real for me or not? Am I going to go with this or not?

VH: I went through that. I came to the Lord as a thirteen-year-old boy out in the country. I got out along the roads and knelt. I don't even remember what I said. Then I would hear some ex-gambler tell about being saved and, you know, it thundered and lightninged, and angels, and everything else. I said, "Lord, if that's what it takes, maybe I haven't got it." I believe a lot of good people have that problem. They have never had an emotional blast.

I asked W. A. Criswell at Dallas, "Is it true you didn't have assurance when you started out preaching?" "Yep, that's right," he said. "I'd be preaching in the morning and be on my knees at night trying to *feel* saved." That's the way he put it. He said, "I finally got to the place where I just said, 'Now, Lord, it says that he that believes on the Son has eternal life, and I do. If I knew how to do it any better, I would. At the judgment day I'm going to say, here is where I stand, Lord.'" By the way he preaches now, he must be sure.

But I believe, don't you, that we have a lot of good folks who love the Lord in their hearts and if they knew what else to do, they'd do it.

JJ: I heard a man speak on a little chart about fact, faith, and feeling. He said feeling comes last. Fact is there whether you feel it or not. Even if you don't have faith, whether you accept it, Christ died for your sins. First is the fact, then you have faith in it, and then the feeling might come. That really settled it for me. I decided I didn't have to *feel* anything.

VH: I'm glad to hear you say that. Alexander Whyte told someone that out in the wilderness when Moses lifted up the serpent, there were several hundred thousand people there. The fellow in the back row couldn't even see the snake, let alone make out the image. Whyte said, "God didn't say see, He said look."

JJ: Somebody said, in fact I think it was *Time* magazine, that American Christians love to be preached at and called sinners as long as they are not called on to repent.

VH: They're not going to repent until they are convicted and confess and forsake. Trouble today is we want God to forgive us our sins without us forsaking them. Somebody said, "God is not going to remove our sins by forgiving them if we're not willing to forsake them."

One of my books, *The Best of Vance Havner*, sold originally for sixty cents in paper back. I wouldn't have been worth much more than a dollar all told if the best is worth sixty cents.

JJ: What do you like to read?

VH: Well, I don't buy many books that you read and lay down and don't read any more. I try to find something thought provoking. Old A. W. Tozer provokes my thought. I've got everything he has written.

I had a week of meetings in Tozer's church in Chicago years ago. After it was over he said, "Well, thank the Lord for one man I don't clean up after."

JJ: What do you see as the greatest need in the evangelical church right now?

VH: Revival. But as I say, that's come to mean what I don't mean.

JJ: What do *you* mean?

VH: Repentance and the gathering of the assembly of anyone in the churches who means business.

I go around getting kindling wood and hope they'll go home and start a fire in the church with it. And you don't have to have much kindling wood to start a big fire.

You know I get a better response from young people today than I have ever had in all these years.

JJ: Interesting.

VH: Yes, sir, I try to keep current and old-fashioned both. Have you heard about the best thing for fat folks?

JJ: No.

VH: Eat garlic sandwiches. It won't affect the fat, but you'll look smaller at a distance.

JJ: Ouch.

VH: Isn't that awful?

One of the besetting sins of old men is to talk too long. Reminiscing, you know. Nobody gives a hoot about all that. You get to wandering around forty years ago and all that sort of business. May sound good to you, but you don't want to stand up there and enjoy your own preaching while everybody else is bored to death.

I don't preach very long as a rule. If you stick to your notes you won't wander much.

JJ: Do you long for the day when you can go to heaven?

VH: Like George Palmer said before he died, "I'm homesick for heaven." It's the hope of dying that has kept me alive this long. That's the way it is with me.

JJ: What would you want as your epitaph?

VH: I think, apart from any verse of Scripture, I would settle for Just a Preacher.

## SEPTEMBER 2, 1973

You haven't lost anything when you know where it is. Death can hide but not divide.

# September 2, 1973

Mrs. Havner passed away at 2:15 this morning. I had not prepared this message with that in mind, but I think that you will perceive how pertinent it is.

If our faith doesn't help us in such a time, it is not worth having any time.

We are all familiar with the beatitudes in the Sermon on the Mount, and others such as "Blessed is that servant, whom his lord when he cometh shall find so doing" (Luke 12:43) and "Blessed are they that hear the Word of God and keep it" (Luke 11:28). But in the eleventh chapter of Matthew we have a little beatitude we are in serious danger of overlooking. I call it "The Forgotten Beatitude."

John the Baptist was in prison. That rugged, ascetic Elijah of the New Testament, that outdoor preacher, was out of place in a damp, cold dungeon. No wonder he had the blues.

One day, he hit such a record low that he sent a delegation to the Lord Jesus and asked, "Art Thou He that should come, or do we look for another?" (Matthew 11:3).

Now, that was an awful thing for John to say. What he had preached like a living exclamation point on the banks of the Jordan had become a question mark to the preacher himself. Now that's not the first time a preacher's affirmation has turned to an interrogative in a dungeon. Jeremiah said to God, "Wilt thou be altogether unto me like a liar, and as waters that fail?" (Jeremiah 15:18).

John had preached a victorious Messiah who would come with His fan in His hand, gathering the wheat into the garner and burning the chaff with unquenchable fire. But here was the Lord Jesus, not like that at all. Meek, lowly, and doing

19

good, He didn't fit the picture; and here in this dungeon of doubt John fell into depression and despair. This man who could reprove kings and call religious people snakes could get in the dumps even as you and I.

It's one thing to stand on Jordan and give it. It's another thing to stay in jail and take it.

But my Lord didn't reprimand this troubled prophet. He didn't say, "I'm ashamed of you. I'm disappointed in you. I'm going to get a new herald and announcer." He didn't send him a cute little tract on how to be happy in jail.

To the contrary. On the very day John made the poorest remark he ever made about Jesus, the Lord said the finest thing that He ever said about John: "Among them that are born of women there hath not risen a greater" (Matthew 11:11).

Our Lord knew his frame and remembered John was dust. So He sent this word to John: "The blind receive their sight, and the lame walk, the lepers are cleansed, and the deaf hear, the dead are raised up, and the poor have the gospel preached to them. And *blessed is he, whosoever shall not be offended in me*" (Matthew 11:5-6, italics added). "Blessed is he whomsoever shall not get upset by the way I run My business." That's just about what it amounts to.

" 'I'm running on schedule,' tell him. 'I'm carrying out My program.' Tell him not to be upset just because I'm not doing it the way he expected."

Now, beloved, we're living in the day of dungeons, and many a Christian is in the clutches of despair. If a husky heart like John the Baptist could faint, then "think it not strange concerning the fiery trial which is to try you, as though some strange thing happened unto you" (1 Peter 4:12).

Are you in a dungeon today? Is it bad health, financial trouble, blood pressure up, and bank account down? You prayed and your prayer wasn't answered. You gave your tithe and everybody said you'd prosper, but now you have less than you had. You prayed for your children and they are worldlings, all fallen apart; while across the street there is an ungodly family with all of theirs intact.

Does your heart lie buried in a grave this morning? Has everything been taken away and you say, "Lord, I just don't understand"?

Now depression brings doubt, and doubt brings despair. Are you offended in Jesus?

Well, that's nothing. He was always offending somebody. He offended more people than anybody who has ever lived. Isaiah 8:14 says He is either a sanctuary or a stumbling stone. He offended His own nation (Romans 9:33). He offended the Pharisees (Matthew 15:12). He offended the people of his own hometown (Matthew 13:54-58). He offended superficial disciples (John 6:60-66). The cross is an offense (1 Corinthians 1:23).

Can't you imagine John the Baptist saying, "If He can raise the dead, why can't He get me out of jail? Here I am with multitudes to hear me. I could be preaching to throngs."

But my Lord delivered Peter from jail and left John the Baptist in there to die. He healed individuals and sometimes left a whole crowd of people unhealed. When Lazarus got sick and they sent an SOS to Jesus to hurry, He just didn't do it. He stayed on two days where He was. When He did get there, poor Martha said, "If you had been here, this wouldn't have happened. He wouldn't have died." But the delay brought a greater miracle than speedy action would have done.

Oh, I think about a precious song we don't sing enough: "Spirit of God, Descend upon My Heart"—"I ask no dream, no prophet ecstacies, / No sudden rending of the veil of clay, / No angel visitant, no op'ning skies; / But take the dimness of my soul away." And then that fourth verse has been getting hold of me for a long time—"Teach me to feel that Thou art always nigh; / Teach me the struggles of the soul to bare, / To check the rising doubt, the rebel sigh; / Teach me the patience of unanswered prayer."

Now, whoever wrote that had been further along than some

of the saints have been today. I get a little weary of these dear souls who have all the dealing and doing of Providence catalogued and correlated and figured out and can give you glib little answers to your heartache. They haven't been far. God just doesn't operate on our time table. And some of His operations don't add up on our computers.

The little boy who didn't understand why God put so many vitamins in spinach and didn't put more of them in ice cream had a pretty good idea that it just doesn't work out like you'd think.

Our Lord announced His program in Nazareth in Luke 4:18. His text there sounds very much like His message to John the Baptist:

"The Spirit of the Lord is upon me, because he hath anointed me to preach the gospel to the poor; he hath sent me to heal the brokenhearted, to preach deliverance to the captives, and recovering of sight to the blind, to set at liberty them that are bruised"—the four *B*'s.

Others are in the dungeon of disillusionment today, and they're saying, "Why doesn't God do something? If Jesus Christ is the Prince of Peace, King of kings, and Lord of lords, why doesn't He come down here and clean up this mess?"

John the Baptist had preached Jesus as both the Lamb of God and as the coming Messiah who would set things right. He is still among us as the Lamb, still reconciling the world to Himself. When the cup of iniquity is full, when lawlessness reaches its climax, when the fullness of the Gentiles has come in, He'll return as a Lion. He'll return for retribution, not reconciliation. He'll set up His kingdom, establish law and order, rule with a rod of iron. Nature will be at peace. Evil will be under control. And we'll all be down by the riverside, singing "Ain't Gonna Study War No More."

So don't be discouraged in a dungeon. If you're tempted to wonder, "Art Thou He that should come or look we for another?" remember He is running on schedule. Claim the forgotten beatitude.

I have made up my mind—and I did it before 2:15 this morning—that however God does it will be all right with me. And you'd better come to that decision.

The Lord tested the disciples on this very point. In John 6 the crowds left Him after He preached a great sermon. Some sermons, you know, do drive the crowd away. When everybody left except the disciples, He turned to them and said, "Will ye also go away?" (John 6:67).

And Peter said, "Lord, to whom shall we go?" (v. 68). "Where would we go, Lord?"

(That's the number one reason I am here this morning after my wife died. Where else would I go?)

Second, Peter said, "Thou hast the words of eternal life" (v. 68). He didn't understand all of them; but he knew that, if the Lord planted them, they would sprout.

And the best reason comes last: "And we believe and are sure that Thou art that Christ, the Son of the living God" (v. 69). We not only believe it, we know it.

Do you believe it, or do you know it? You can believe it and not know it. You can believe it up in your head and not know it down in your heart.

I personally am not looking for another. My Christ has already come, and I am looking for Him to come back. In the meantime He is still doing what He came to do the first time. I don't understand all He does and why He does it. But if the devil thought that by what I have been through in the last five months with my wife he was going to shake my faith and get me into the dungeon to be a partner with John the Baptist in saying, "Are you the one?" then he overshot the mark.

Even in the dungeon, I am not looking for another. I have found in Him not a stumbling block but a sanctuary. Now I claim the blessing of the unoffended and the forgotten beatitude.

My Sarah in the last two days of her life managed to write a few things that I could read. She had no other way of communication with those gadgets in her mouth. And one of them said, "I am having to endure what I cannot tell you on paper."

I had been preaching a sermon on living in the great "Until." I don't know if that was in her mind or not, but the thought did me a lot of good. Until. Until the fullness of the Gentiles is come in. Until the times of the Gentiles be fulfilled. Until the Lord returns. I am living this morning for "Until."

Over in London during the Second World War, when Hitler was blitzing London with his air force, the English loaded train after train with children and moved them out to the country, evacuating them for safety.

Somebody asked one little youngster, "Where are you going?"

He said, "I don't know, but the king knows."

There may come a time when your train, too, takes off for some strange destination. I don't know where I am going from here. But my King knows. I don't know what the rest of my ministry is going to be like. It is sort of overwhelming if you try to figure that out, when you have lost your standby—humanly speaking.

But then, I haven't lost her because I know where she is. You haven't lost anything when you know where it is. Death can hide but not divide. Thou art gone to Christ's other side. Thou art with Christ, and Christ with me. We're united still in Christ.

So don't you ever say, when your dear one goes, "I've lost her," or, "I've lost him." If you are in the Lord and he or she was in the Lord, you know where they are. We're only apart—until—He comes. We are living in the great "Until."

We have an old saying that you never miss the water until the well goes dry. Now, I want to say to you that one of the greatest sins of all is our taking things—America, the church, health, loved ones—for granted. Now, aren't you guilty this morning? Aren't we all? And then there comes a day when you'd give everything you have for just one ordinary day that you had back there—that you took for granted.

You wives and husbands still have that privilege of living another day together. Don't take it for granted. I have thanked God through my regrets that Sarah and I had a wonderful time. We did not take it for granted.

There are times when you are inclined to think this is kind of a dull, drab day and that life gets sort of ordinary. The time will come when you'd give anything for the drabbest day you ever had with the one you loved. And that is so true of my land, America. And it is so true of the church we just take for granted, saying that there's one on almost every other corner and so what.

We take health for granted until we're flat on our backs in the hospital. I've been there all these months. I've been soaked and saturated in hospitals until I've come to a new perspective on a lot of things. I watched dying folks and said, "God have mercy on me that I fail to thank You for being able to move around yet."

And there's the gospel. I take it for granted. And the grace of God, too.

God help us.

The rich man in hell had taken for granted all the things that he'd enjoyed in life. You talk about never missing the water until the well goes dry. What did he want in hell? He wanted water. He didn't want a drink of water. He said, "Could you send somebody who would dip his finger in water? Just one drop for my tongue."

And if you think that is a hideous picture of hell, it is from our Lord—from the meek and lowly Jesus. It is terrible there. Jesus told me about it, or I wouldn't know it. There was a man who missed the opportunity of a lifetime to know God. Now he is reduced. His money is all back of him, and here he is in torment, my Lord says. All he wants is a drop of water (Luke 16:19-31).

If you are outside the grace of God in salvation, I beg you in God's name to receive the Lord Jesus as your Savior. You may be a church member. You may think you are pretty well fixed. You're comfortable. You're satisfied. But if you don't know Jesus, I can only tell you what He said. He painted the most hideous picture of the life to come for the unsaved that is to be found anywhere.

When I pastored a country church, a farmer didn't like sermons I preached on hell. He said, "Preach about the meek and lowly Jesus."

I said, "That's where I got my information about hell."

Don't take for granted the things that God has blessed you with. Above all, don't take for granted the gift of His Son.

You prayed for me so diligently during these past months, and I've appreciated it so much. I don't understand and you don't understand why our prayers weren't answered in the way we'd hoped.

But it may be that in preaching to other people who go through the same experiences I may be able to do more good than if this thing had come out gloriously with Sarah restored and us traveling the country together. That doesn't happen too often—not after what she'd been through.

But what I'm talking about this morning *does* happen pretty often. And it may happen to you.

If it can be used of God to fortify your heart—in your dungeon, in your extremity—then it won't have been in vain.

## ON THIS ROCK I STAND

I feel like American humorist Josh Billings, who said, "I'd rather know a few things for certain than be sure of a lot of things that ain't so."

# On This Rock I Stand

*If the foundations be destroyed, what can the right-eous do* (Psalm 11:3)?
*For other foundation can no man lay than that is laid, which is Jesus Christ* (1 Corinthians 3:11).

Years ago, when the Democratic convention nominated William Jennings Bryan for the presidency, some of the delegates were rather let down because he wasn't well known. One rather disconsolate Democrat was approached by someone who asked him, "Are you still a Democrat?"

He answered, "Yes, and very still."

I sometimes think of that man as I make my way through a world that has become a madhouse. I feel like saying in the midst of all this bedlam, "No comment."

My wife and I were taking a bus trip through the mountains, and the bus broke down right in front of a hillbilly grocery store. The woman there apparently had never been anywhere else much.

My wife said, "I don't believe she knows what's going on in the world outside."

I said, "Well, don't tell her. I wouldn't want the poor soul to know. Let her die in peace."

But we must not keep silent in an evil time. I speak as an individual and not as a representative of any clique or group or movement. I'm an American by birth and a Christian by second birth. I'm not interested in theological fads that change like women's fashions, and by which spiritual adolescents and the immature are carried away by every wind of doctrine. I'm tired of reading about neo-orthodoxy and neo-evangelicalism

29

and neo-Romanism and neo-Universalism and neo-everything else.

I'm tired of hootenanny religion, the new brand of Christianity that pagans do not feel embarrassed to join. I'm tired of Batman, the Beatniks, the Beatles, the "God is dead" movement, the new morality, situation ethics, existentialism, and the latest theological abberation out of Germany. If my faith were so weak that a professor down in Georgia could shake it, I'd get another kind.

I'm tired of hearing in our church bodies that we must get away from our humble beginnings, shake the hayseed out of our hair, and come of age. I hear a lot today about grandstand seats in glory, but I don't hear much about the baptism of Christ's sufferings. We're wearing a lot of medals these days and not many scars.

I'm tired of modern efforts to force a counterfeit kingdom of God on an unregenerate society. I'm tired of schemes to bring in the Millennium by education, legislation, and reformation. They sweep out the house only to have seven devils return and the last state become worse than the first.

I'm tired of all the tricks by which we try to make moral issues out of political projects. I'm tired of our bragging about how sophisticated we are, when actually we are the most gullible of generations. We've bought more gold bricks and white elephants than any crowd that has lived since Adam.

I'm tired of the new freedom that throws the Ten Commandments out the window and doesn't know the difference between love and lust. My Bible still reads, "Thou shalt not commit adultery," but now we have situation ethics and the new immorality. Even churches take such a stand. Over in England, Billy Graham said he never thought he'd see the day when religious leaders would make it easy for young people to break the moral law of God.

We read, "Thou shalt not steal," but shoplifters alone over Christmas steal more than 600 million dollars worth of goods.

There's no regard for the law of God. I heard of a family on a picnic some time ago. When the boy stole a watermelon out of a patch nearby, his mother said, "Don't you get another one. You don't know what they've been sprayed with."

Love does not annul the Ten Commandments. Love obeys them. Love has no other gods. Love does not worship graven images. Love does not take God's name in vain. Love keeps the Lord's Day and honors father and mother. It does not commit adultery, does not steal, kill, bear false witness, or covet.

I'm tired of the professors who brainwash young students into disbelieving the Word of God. I'm tired of popular commentaries that doubt or deny every miracle in the Book. I'm tired of seeing the Stars and Stripes dragged in the dust, the great heroes of the past smeared, and patriotism junked in favor of an internationalism that's part of the program of Antichrist.

I'm tired of hearing sin called sickness and alcoholism a disease. It's the only disease I know of that we're spending hundreds of millions of dollars a year to spread. Everybody's sick. Nowadays a liar is just an extrovert with a lively imagination. A murderer is just a victim of a traumatic experience; his mother wouldn't let him push his oatmeal dish off the tray when he was little, so now he pushes his wife off Brooklyn Bridge. We recognize adultery in the slums, but not in Hollywood. Illegitimacy has become respectable and is subsidized by the welfare state.

I'm tired of experts who know all the answers when they don't even know what the question is. I'm tired of all this excitement about living on the moon when we have never learned how to live on the earth. We are not going to last long enough morally to do what we are trying to do scientifically.

I'm tired of artificial wealth by which America is riding to the poorhouse in a Cadillac. I'm tired of this joke called progress. We've learned how to lengthen life, but we don't know how to deepen it. You would have to live twice as long to live half as much as your fathers. Somebody has said birthdays tell how long you've been on the road, but not how far you've traveled.

Then we have wonder drugs. You take them and wonder what's going to happen. The misuse and the long-range effects of those drugs raise problems as great as they solve.

I'm tired of wading through secondhand tobacco smoke from a generation of lung cancer prospects, while the surgeon general warns the nation and pulpits keep silent. I hear about "I'd rather fight than switch," but what bothers me is this crowd that would rather die than quit.

I'm tired of hearing about temperance instead of abstinence, in order to please the cocktail crowd in church congregations.

We've polluted the very air we breathe till we wheeze our way through the smog. We've polluted the water until our rivers have become sewers. Our cities have become jungles of crime where no decent woman walks the streets at night. We live in a madhouse of ear-splitting noise that's become a national problem. The experts tell us that city dwellers soon will have to wear gas masks and hearing aids.

We don't know how to be quiet these days. I grew up far from the madding crowd's ignoble strife. Those country people lived their simple lives next to the wonders of God's beautiful world. We met at the little country church for our revival meetings in the summertime, went out for dinner at each other's homes, and had time to sit on the front porch and talk all afternoon.

My father's home was the staying place for the preachers in the horse-and-buggy days. We had only one sermon a month—some of them were long enough to last a month. Father would let me sit up late on Saturday night before the open fire, while he and the minister talked long and late about the things of God. They built a wall *around* my soul that the world, the flesh, and the devil could not breach, and deposited a sediment of conviction *in* my soul that has stood the test of the years. We had time to be still and to think. But there is no such time today.

Of all the illusions and fantasies and farces of human history, the biggest mirage of all is what we call progress. Just because we split the atom and are back from the moon, we've given God His walking papers. We have decided we can work out our own salvation, and that science has the answer to sin.

The Scriptures tell us that history will end in catastrophe, abounding lawlessness, abating love, perilous times in a world that's lost its way. There is not one area of life today—government, law, common safety, morality, national debt, world peace, air pollution, traffic, family life, art, literature, theology—that is not in one hopeless mess. We've boxed ourselves in, locked the door, and thrown away the key.

I read of a doctor who all his life took a stand on a certain medical issue that brought a laugh from his fellow doctors, until it was discovered that he was right and they were wrong. Somebody said he was wrong so long that he turned out to be right. Some of us have been accustomed to being laughed at by certain swivel chair experts in eschatology, but when God splits the skies and the stars fall, the moon turns to blood and men cry for rocks and mountains to fall on them, it's going to be pretty hard for some of us to keep from saying, "I told you so."

We've invented television, but what is there worth televising? We have computers to do our thinking, but who is thinking? We have more leisure, but how do we use it? Men used to have visions of God. Now they see another world only when they eat a sugar cube of LSD.

Well, if there are some things I'm tired of, are there some things I'm sure about? Yes, my friend, I'm sure about a few things. I feel like American humorist Josh Billings who said, "I'd rather know a few things for certain than be sure of a lot of things that ain't so." I know a few things for certain.

I believe the Bible is the Word of God. I don't understand it all, but I stand on it. It does not need our vindication, although the archaeologist's spade digs up evidence every day to shut the mouths of critics. They've buried the Bible like

34

they've tried to bury God, but the corpse always comes to life in the midst of the interment, to outlive all the pallbearers.

They tell us today that the creation story and the virgin birth and the resurrection are not miracles; they are myths. If I thought all those blessed truths were just myths, I'd be mythtified, and mythtaken, and mytherable.

> What more can He say than to you He hath said,
> To you who for refuge to Jesus have fled?*

And on that rock I stand.

I believe Jesus Christ is the Son of God. I believe He was born of the virgin Mary; otherwise, He would have been born out of wedlock, and I'm not interested in that kind of Savior. They say that the virgin birth is recorded only in Luke, although I don't agree with that; but if it were recorded only once, how many times does God have to say it before we believe it? I believe the record God gave of His Son. And on that rock I stand.

I believe Jesus Christ died for my sins. He didn't come down here merely to teach, to be an example, to die a martyr. He came to do something about our main problem, which includes all other problems. You would never know it is the main problem today. Nobody in Congress is going to stand up and say the trouble is sin; nobody in the UN, nobody in the universities, nobody in the scientific laboratories, nobody in world capitals. We are all trying to sweep out the cobwebs, and nobody says anything about the spider. But that spider is sin, and Jesus Christ died for our sins according to the Scriptures. That is the record, and on that rock I stand.

I believe Jesus Christ rose bodily from the grave. I'm not worshiping a ghost. The world knows that He died, and the church believes He rose. He could have appeared to Herod and Pilate and put on a demonstration in Jerusalem. He could have been the greatest sensation of all time; but He revealed Himself only to His disciples. We have the greatest secret

*"How Firm a Foundation."

of all times, and the church is the greatest secret keeper of all times. I accept the fact of the resurrection. I've entered into the experience of it. I'm living in the power of it. I'm awaiting the final fulfillment of it. And on that rock I stand.

I believe Jesus Christ is coming back personally and visibly to reign on earth, and the sooner the better. When He came the first time, neither the Roman world of government, nor the Greek world of culture, nor the Hebrew world of religion would receive Him. And when He comes back, neither government, culture, nor religion will hang out a welcome sign. Even the church is so busy puttering around down here that she scarcely lifts her eyes toward heaven to pray, "Even so, come, Lord Jesus."

Wouldn't you think that it would be on all our lips? Wouldn't you think it would be the subject of many a happy conversation? You try bringing up the matter of the Lord's return in many a fellowship of church members and see how suspicious and hesitant they seem, how embarrassed. The Lord's return is the unwanted stepchild in the family of church doctrine in many an area today. But on that rock I stand.

I believe the church, the true church, is the good society of all people who have been born twice. I'm not talking about that ecclesiastical octopus, the world church, which along with the world state is shaping up before our eyes and will end under Antichrist. That will be the only church officially recognized in that day. But there is another church whose statistics are in heaven, whose fellowship is in the Spirit, whose foundation is Jesus Christ. On that rock I stand.

There is still a remnant of good, humble, hard-working, grass-roots people in America who are tired of a lot of things going on. I meet them everywhere. They grip my hand. Some don't speak out as they ought. They're afraid of being identified with odd-ball, off-brand groups they wouldn't be caught dead in—groups who happen to believe some of the same things they believe.

My Bible says the devils believe there is a God and tremble.

Well, that is one place where the devil and I agree. But I'm not renouncing the old simplicities just because some crackpots twist them to suit their purposes.

I believe Jesus Christ is the answer to every problem—past, present, and future. By Him all things consist, and we are complete in Him. F-A-I-T-H spells out into "For-All-I-Take-Him." For all my need I trust him. For all His blessings I thank Him. I believe that all who trust Him will have eternal life, and that all who reject Him will live in conscious torment forever. I believe there is a hell.

Most of the information that I have about hell I got from Jesus. He took the last verse of Isaiah and the garbage heap outside Jerusalem and mixed them up into the most fearful picture of eternal punishment on earth. I've read books and heard sermons trying to say that my Lord's belief in hell was an accommodation to the ideas of His time. But no amount of exegetical sleight of hand can change the fact that He saw the future abode of the wicked as endless horror beyond the great gulf that was forever fixed. I believe there is a hell because He did. And on that rock I stand.

I believe there is a heaven. One day, when I was a little boy in western North Carolina, I carved an inscription on one of the bricks of the old-fashioned chimney of my home. It read, "Heaven I hope to win." I had been told at home and in the little country church and at Sunday school about a beautiful city. They had read *Pilgrim's Progress* to me, and I had made up my mind to head heavenward.

Not long ago I visited that old spot where the plain little house and the old chimney still stand. I searched for that inscription on the worn old brick, and to my delight I found it. Carved over half a century ago, most of it had been erased by the rains and the snows and the steady erosion of heat and cold. But I could still make out clearly two words—*heaven* and *hope*.

I, too, have stood the gales, the summers, the winters of all those years, but the ravages of life's seasons have not removed the hope of heaven from my heart. It is embedded there more securely than my boyish fingers ever carved it into that old brick. The infidels have blown their blast, and Bible critics even in pulpits and seminary chairs have tried to dim that hope. But it burns brighter than ever before.

When I wrote that inscription, most of my loved ones were living here. Now most of them have taken up their residence over there. But best of all, I have my Savior's word about it: "If it were not so, I would have told you" (John 14:2). That settles it. If it weren't true, He would let us know. And on that rock I stand.

Now, you say, that's old-fashioned. Yes, and so is the sun. But without it, men grope in darkness. So is air, but without it men gasp and die. So is water, and without it men go mad. How dependent we are on simple things in spite of all our gadgetry and technology.

You remember the power failure in New York. Millions of people sat in the great city just waiting for the sun to rise.

They had some unusual smog out in Los Angeles some time ago, and one of the top meteorologists said that only a sweep of wind from elsewhere would relieve it. They were there, waiting for the wind to blow.

There was a drought, and all the agricultural experts and weathermen were at wits' end, just waiting for plain, old-fashioned rain. So for all his science and gadgets and gimmicks, man is a helpless creature, depending on the sun, air, and water—just as always.

Some time ago, two Indians who had been watching a light-house go up came over to see the thing open on the big day. It was all set up with the lights and the bell and the horn; but the day it was due to open, the worst fog of all fogs came in.

One Indian said to the other, "Light shine, bell ring, horn blow, but fog come in just the same."

We've never had more lights shining, and bells ringing, and horns blowing in the church than we have today. We've never had more fog.

The greatest hindrance to many a man's salvation is not his badness, but his goodness—the good that is not good enough. "Except your righteousness shall exceed the righteousness of the scribes and Pharisees . . ." Well, now, that righteousness was pretty good. They went to the Lord's house and read the Bible. They tithed and lived separated lives. They were ahead of most of our church members today. But it wasn't good enough. Education is good, but it isn't good enough. Moral character is good, but it isn't good enough. Reformation is good, but it isn't good enough. Church membership is good, but it isn't good enough.

> There is a green hill far away,
>    Without a city wall,
> Where the dear Lord was crucified,
>    Who died to save us all.
> There was no other good enough
>    To pay the price of sin;
> He only could unlock the gate
>    Of heaven and let us in.*

Long ago, one of England's greatest preachers, Joseph Parker, preached a mighty sermon on the stupidity of the specialists. His text was from 1 Peter 2 concerning the stone which the builders rejected—the builders of all people, mind you—the experts, the specialists. This is the age of the expert. Our civilization is crumbling because the experts have rejected the only foundation that will endure. All other ground is sinking sand.

"Other foundation can no man lay than that is laid, which is Jesus Christ" (1 Corinthians 3:11). On that rock I stand.

*Cecil F. Alexander.

## IT'S ABOUT TIME

It's about time we quit playing church in these services that start at eleven o'clock sharp and end at twelve o'clock dull.

# It's About Time

It is the irony of ironies that with the most elaborate time-keeping devices we have ever had—we wear sophisticated watches, we have clocks everywhere, we keep current with events on television—yet there has never been a generation as ignorant of the answer to one little question: "What time is it?"

I have an old Book, God's timepiece, and it has been ticking for centuries. Sometimes it has seemed slow, but it has never been late. It is a clock set by God Almighty. Heaven and earth may pass away, but it will not. And bless God, it is on Standard Time. And woe unto us if we try to set it back or push it forward.

You will find that if you dig into it, you will have the sensation an electrician gets when he rewires an old house where the power has not been cut off. You will get a shock. It has its own alarm, too, and God have mercy on the man who turns it off or sleeps through its warning.

But one thing is certain. It is later than we think, and only God knows what time it is. Psalm 119:126 says, "It is time for thee, Lord, to work: for they have made void thy law."

Civilization today reminds me of an ape with a blowtorch playing in a room full of dynamite. It looks like the monkeys are about to operate the zoo, and the inmates are taking over the asylum. We have painted ourselves into a corner and have become victims of the scientific monster we have created.

Somebody has said that what American youth need today is a new hero—that we really have not had one since Lindbergh. Oh, the men who went to the moon performed a far more difficult feat, but we do not remember their names as we do

41

the youngster who sat down in that crate of an airplane with no radio—no anything—and took off for Paris. He had to have a lot of something that most of us do not have.

But after it was over, of course, the world was at his feet. He was an idol everywhere. Folks were so excited! Even sober President Calvin Coolidge got excited. And that lasted for a while. But soon Lindy grew tired of all that adulation and fame. Then tragedy came along in the kidnapping and murder of his baby boy. He moved over to England to live and hobnobbed some with the Nazis.

Franklin D. Roosevelt called him a traitor, but later on, President Eisenhower promoted him. He served in World War II in an advisory capacity. Then he became interested in conservation and later discovered that he had a terminal illness. And in his characteristic fashion, he planned his own funeral. They buried him in a fatigue outfit in a plain grave in Hawaii, where he lived. I do not believe he was even embalmed. On his tombstone appear the words, "Though I mount up with the wings of the morning."

But Lindy said this, "I have lived to see the science I worshiped and the aircraft I loved destroying the civilization I expected them to serve." That tells us something of the disillusionment of that remarkable man. And the world has something of that attitude today. All our grand inventions have gotten us into a predicament somehow. The experts have all the answers, but even they do not know what the question is.

I sat up three hours one night, watching television—which is a record for me. But I could not stop. I was watching William L. Schirer's presentation of the rise and fall of the Third Reich, the career of Adolph Hitler. And as I watched that maniac, that demoniac, that queer, strange character, standing before multitudes of Germans as far as the eye could see, I realized there was a man with hypnotic power that would make a nation as grand and wonderful and literate as Germany turn over its youth, its money, its government, its everything to him.

Arnold Toynbee could not understand that. The great historian could not figure why a nation like Germany would let a wild man like Hitler almost wreck not only Germany, but the whole world. He arrived at a conclusion that sounds like a preacher's: "There must be a vein of original sin in human nature. Civilization is only a thin cake of custom overlying a molten mass of wickedness always boiling up for an opportunity to burst out."

There is only one explanation for the moral mess we are in worldwide—and it is the worst we have been in since Adam and Eve ate us out of house and home in the Garden of Eden. You will not hear much about the real cause from Washington, Congress, or the United Nations. You won't hear about it in universities or scientific centers.

The cause of the trouble is that we have made void the law of God.

The Lord God omnipotent reigneth, and He has given us physical, moral, and spiritual laws. We may not like the way some of them operate, but that is the way it is. God made marriage and the home the basis of society; and the people that live together today without getting married need to learn that that is not the way it is. Be not deceived; God is not mocked.

You cannot break the laws of God. Nobody ever broke the laws of God. You break yourself against them. You might as well try to attack Gibraltar with a popgun as go up against the laws of God. You jump off a skyscraper, and you do not break the law of gravity. You break your neck, but not the law of gravity.

My Lord said lawlessness would abound and love would abate. You are foolish if you think you can be immoral and escape the consequences. Now there are all kinds of devices today to avoid the results, but none to avoid the consequences: diseased bodies, cooked brains, blasted lives, broken homes, and suicides. This is a day when we think we have made void

God's law, and we think we can get away with it.

Homosexuality, pornography, drugs, streets not safe to walk on day or night, homes unsafe!

When I was growing up in the foothills of the Blue Ridge Mountains in western North Carolina, we had our revival in the summertime at the little church up the road. We never locked up the house to go to a meeting. Nobody would break in. It was safe. The other day I was in a motel where they had the telephone screwed to the table.

You heard about the woman who said, "What are we coming to? Somebody broke into my house and stole all of my Holiday Inn towels!"

I was in a motel the other day that had a little notice up just for fun, but it had a point. It said, "We will now accept dogs. We have not admitted dogs, but we can have dogs stay here now." It said, "After all, no dog ever set the place on fire with a cigarette. No dog ever went out without paying his bill. No dog ever stole our blankets."

Then it had a little notice down underneath that was for us folks: "If you can get your dog to vouch for you, we'll let you stay here too." We are in a bad way when we have to get the endorsement of a dog to stay somewhere.

And yet, on the other hand, there is a dramatically serious side to this strange paradox of progress. I was in Jacksonville for meetings when the last group of astronauts landed on the moon. I could watch on the television in the corner, and then I could look out the window into the park where I dared not walk. We're smart enough to walk on the moon, but not safe enough to walk in the park.

That is the paradox of progress today. There is no room in the jails for the criminals if they could even be caught. There is no time to try them. The dockets are full. Capital punishment is frowned on, although God Almighty started it. Authority is no longer recognized in home, school, or church.

Some time ago, a school principal said to the teachers, "Don't tell the students to obey. That's out. Tell them to cooperate, but not obey." Now *cooperate* is not the word my daddy used when I was growing up. If I had not cooperated, he would have operated, you can be sure of that.

We have made void the law of God.

You see it in every realm. You see it in surrealistic and modern art. I heard of one picture that was by mistake hung upside down in an art exhibit and won the prize. And then there is rock and roll. I have never called it music. It's just an excuse for not being able to make music.

And then there is the liquor business that was once denounced from the pulpit. Now the clergy has kind words for cocktails because so many of the congregation drink them. Total abstinence is considered Victorian and puritanical. We discuss what to do about alcoholism, but nobody seems to want to do much about alcohol. And that is simply a matter of trying to mop up the floor while you leave the faucet running.

There is only one answer to this dilemma today, and it is in my text: "It is time for thee, Lord, to work: for they have made void thy law." It's about time for God to intervene to straighten out the iniquities and inequities of this Sodom and Gomorrah. It is time for God to judge this generation that has laughed in His face, pronounced Him dead, denied His Word, disowned His Son, and turned His holy day into a holiday. It's time for God to show up our blind leaders of the blind— and what is worse, our bland leaders of the bland, who go about dusting off sin with a powder puff and spreading cold cream on cancers.

It's about time for our younger generation to turn to that old verse in the old Book: "Rejoice, O young man, in thy youth; and let thy heart cheer thee in the days of thy youth, and walk in the ways of thine heart, and in the sight of thine eyes: but know thou, that for all these things God will bring thee into judgment" (Ecclesiastes 11:9).

I have been preaching for more than sixty-five years, but I get a better response today from young people than ever before. All this talk about the communication gap is a lot of eyewash. When young people feel you are genuine, and you speak with authority, and you lay it on the line, most of them will respond. I am amazed at the number of subteenagers, little folks, that come up sometimes after a message and make intelligent comments about the sermon.

It's time for all of us, young and old, to seek the Lord. Too many churches have begun in the Spirit and are trying to perfect themselves in the flesh. Methods have been borrowed from the world. David is hauling the Ark on a new cart these days. The spirit of the shop has invaded the sanctuary. Preachers' studies have become offices, and corporation methods have taken the place of consecrated men. Human busyness has supplanted the Father's business.

I like the homely phrases in my old Bible. I like, "Break up your fallow ground." Most folks—especially if you grew up in the country—know that is ground that has lain idle and undisturbed and uncultivated. All it now produces is weeds and briers and brambles. It is not producing anything worthwhile because it is undisturbed.

Human hearts get like that. Jesus told us about four kinds of soil and four kinds of human hearts. Frankly, I wonder whether we shall ever have another deep revival in such a shallow generation. The sharp plow blade must be put deep in the soil if you are going to have any harvest. There must be the breaking up of the fallow ground.

Another homely phrase says that Moab has settled on his lees and has not been emptied from vessel to vessel. The individual church and the individual Christian need to be shaken up and emptied from vessel to vessel. That is what a revival is. It empties the church from vessel to vessel. There is a stirring process.

Sometimes your medicine bottle has on it, "Shake well before using." That is what God has to do with some of His people. He has to shake them well before they are ever usable. Paul wrote to Timothy, "Stir up the gift of God, which is in thee." Do not wait for a lovely feeling to come over you. You do it. Stir up the gift of God that is within you. When the lemonade is still sour, it is because the sugar is at the bottom and needs to be stirred.

I know some dear people who will probably get to heaven when they die, but, my soul, they are not sweet. They do need to be stirred.

I heard of a preacher the other day who was asked, "What's the size of your pastorate?"

He said, "Twenty-five miles wide and one-inch deep." That is what bothers a lot of preachers these days.

When I was a pastor in Charleston, I conducted chapel a number of times at the Citadel. The commandant was General Summerall, who had been Chief of Staff. He was every inch a soldier of the old school. I believe he was a Christian. The sturdy type, he did not say much; and that made what he did say all the more important.

I remember one time after the service, we marched out. I do not get to march with a general often, so I tried to keep in step. When we got out, he wheeled and took my hand and said, "Thank you. You get under these boys' hides."

That is what preaching ought to do. That is what the Word of God does. It ought to get down under that topsoil and do some subsoiling. One type of soil—the stony ground—represents those who enjoy listening to sermons, but somehow the message never gets through to them. It doesn't take root and grow. They know the message is true, and they sort of believe it; but when the hot winds of persecution blow, they lose interest. I've preached to people like that through all these years.

I am amazed at how few people know the difference between a revival and an evangelistic meeting. Revivals don't have a thing to do with sinners, except that evangelism is a product of revival. A revival is a work of the Spirit of God among Christians whereby they get right with God and with each other. Evangelism is preaching the gospel to the lost.

Revival means conviction of sin, confession of sin, forsaking of sin. It is not enough to ask God to take away your sins if you are not willing to put them away. "He that covereth his sins shall not prosper: but whoso confesseth and forsaketh them shall have mercy" (Proverbs 28:13). It means separation from the world. I don't hear much about that anymore. That old subject is out. They have a new word for a lot of things today, and now they call worldliness "secularism." Nobody knows what that is, so that lets the preacher off the hook. He can talk as long as he pleases on secularism and nobody will know what he is talking about.

Revival means submitting to the lordship of Jesus Christ. It means being filled with the Holy Spirit. It does not begin with the backsliders. It begins with the best people in the church—the crowd that is there every Sunday. But it is so hard to get this across to them. It's about time we quit playing church in these services that start at eleven o'clock sharp and end at twelve o'clock dull.

You will never see a revival in a comfortable church.

There is another way God will break through one of these days. The Lord Jesus will come again. Some of us are beginning to feel it's about time.

There is a longing in nature, and I don't think it's just my imagination. Creation groans in pain, the creatures groan, the whole creation stands on tip-toe, "waiting for the manifestation of the sons of God."

A. T. Robertson and some of our finest writers have felt this when they were out in some lovely spot listening to the birds sing. I am a bird-watcher, and when I am in a lonely place and hear a woodthrush singing, I feel the longing of creation for a better day. There is a sense in which the whole creation waits.

One thing that keeps me going these days is not just the hope of dying, but I know that that will mean the redemption of the body and the redemption of creation. I'm waiting. There's a song, "The World Is Waiting for the Sunrise." Better put, the world is waiting for the S-O-N, "Sonrise," when the Son of Righteousness will rise with healing in His wings.

Many years ago, my father and mother put into my hands an old Book. They said, "It'll be a lamp to your feet and a light to your path." There were times when the winds of doubt blew pretty hard. The storms seemed to dampen the glow. Sometimes the darkness was frightening, but that old Light has seen me through to this good hour.

I heard about a camp meeting back in the old days. One night, it looked like a storm was coming up, and they had no lanterns. The preacher had to walk down by a dangerous cliff to where he was staying. So an old farmer got together some "lighters," as we call them in the Blue Ridge Mountains. He got a branch of pine wood, set it on fire, and brought the torch to the preacher.

"This will see you home," he said.

The preacher said, "I don't know about that. What if it rains?"

"It'll see you home."

"But what if the wind blows it out?"

But that farmer knew his pine lighters. "It'll see you home." And it did. "Through many dangers, toils, and snares I have already come."

Once in a while somebody says, "Would you like to live your life over?"

Live my life over when I am this near home? I'm not interested. Who wants to go back? Some of us may leave this life under difficult circumstances, but one thing is certain. God may put some of us to bed in the dark, but He will get us all up in the morning. And that is what I'm looking for. God is up all night. He's always available.

I think of the old bishop who could not sleep, so at two in the morning he got up and started reading his Bible. He came to where it says, "He that keepeth Israel neither slumbers nor sleeps."

He said, "Well, Lord, if You're sitting up, I'm going to bed. Good night."

One of these days, it will be daylight forever. It's about

time. And as we face anarchy in the world and apostasy in the professing church and apathy in the true church, it is about time.

If you do not know the Lord Jesus as your Savior, now is the accepted time; now is the day of salvation.

Our Lord told us about the prosperous farmer who said, "I've got to tear down these old barns and build bigger ones. Then I'm going to say to my soul, 'Take it easy. Thou hast goods laid up for many years.' "

Then God spoke up and said, "You've got the wrong clock. You're going tonight."

There is a lot of difference between "many years" and "tonight." Don't you ever tell your soul to take it easy. That is what is the matter with too may folks now. Get out that old hymnbook and learn how to sing one that has been in moth balls too long:

> Awake, my soul, stretch every nerve,
>   And press with vigor on,
> The heavenly race demands thy zeal
>   And an immortal crown.*

Beloved, it's about time we set our watches with the timekeeper of the universe. A long time ago, my father spoke to a young fellow out there in the country about his soul, and this fellow said, "Well, Mr. Havner, I'm a young man. I've got lots of time, lots of time."

My father was not much for that sort of talk, and he did not brook much foolishness. He answered that boy, but I don't think you would find his approach listed in any book on how to do personal work. He said, "You remind me of a fellow in the Bible that God called a fool."

Three weeks later, that fellow joined a church. They asked, "What brings you here?"

He said, "It started when Mr. Havner said I reminded him of a man in the Bible that God called a fool."

*Philip Doddridge.

Let us end with the admonition of Romans 13, "That, knowing the time, that now it is high time to awake out of sleep: for now is our salvation nearer than when we believed. The night is far spent, the day is at hand: let us therefore cast off the works of darkness, and let us put on the armour of light. Let us walk honestly, as in the day; not in rioting and drunkenness, not in chambering and wantonness, not in strife and envying" (vv. 11-13).

Then comes that double-barreled last verse, 14, that starts with a positive and ends with a negative: "Put ye on the Lord Jesus Christ, and make not provision for the flesh, to fulfill the lusts thereof."

What time is it? It's time for God to work. And it's time to seek the Lord. It's time to wake up.

It's about time.

# THE BETTER OR THE BEST?

Any housewife knows that the best way to remember the things she meant to do and forgot is to start praying. They will come to her mind to divert her from prayer. The devil will let a preacher prepare a sermon if it will keep him from preparing himself.

# The Better or the Best?

Life is a series of choices between the bad and the good and the best. Everything depends on which we choose. Sometimes the alternatives get in each other's way.

It goes without saying that the bad is the enemy of the good. An alarming percentage of God's servants today go down in defeat and disgrace, overcome not by something that is merely doubtful or debatable or borderline, but something downright evil. David was a man after God's own heart, but gross iniquity snared him.

Hollywood may glamorize all that, but God's Word describes such evil as ugly, filthy putrefaction. We are shocked at Christian workers who have to leave town before daylight because their sins have caught up with them. Unmentionable vices, described in Romans 1, break out in the upper brackets of the religious world.

When Paul warned against chambering and wantonness, he had in mind more than meets the eye on first reading. We have grown sentimental about it. We call sickness what God calls sinfulness, and we call weakness what God calls wickedness. Our popular revised code of morality makes immorality respectable. Nothing is bad any more. Evil is applauded, reputations are enhanced, and box office receipts pick up if some celebrities can boast of several licentious escapades.

Every day, there are weird and fantastic crimes committed by children not yet in their teens. Downright vicious evil wrecks multitudes of Christians and plays havoc with many a church.

I will not take my congregation for granted. A Sunday morning congregation is just about the most innocent looking aggregation on the face of the earth; but before I get through many a meeting, moral corruption has been confessed (often by church officers), corruption that nobody dreamed could possibly exist.

You cannot play with this world and not be contaminated. "Be not deceived: evil communications corrupt good manners. Awake to righteousness, and sin not; for some have not the knowledge of God: I speak this to your shame" (1 Corinthians 15:33-34). The Lord's sheep have no business in back alleys with the devil's goats. "Is this vile world a friend to grace, to help me on to God?"

"Let him that thinketh he standeth take heed lest he fall" (1 Corinthians 10:12). Romans 7:4 says that we are married to Christ. Jame 4:4, speaking to church members, says, "Ye adulterers and adulteresses, know ye not that the friendship of the world is enmity with God? whosoever therefore will be a friend of the world is the enemy of God."

No decent married man dates another woman, and no true Christian dates this world. To flirt with it is to fall in love with it and live in spiritual adultery. Physical adultery often begins with a look and casual conversation that is innocent enough. Christians are lured way from the Lord gradually. The first flirtations are sometimes so harmless that warnings are ridiculed. Preachers are called pharisaical, and parents are called puritanical when they warn of danger.

But one thing leads to another, and soon it is too late. The best rule is, do not make the first date. A lot of churches today, for all their new buildings, do not need bowling rooms as much as they need bawling rooms where adulterous members need to weep in repentance over their unfaithfulness to Almighty God.

Not only is the bad the enemy of the best, but there is a sense in which the best may be the enemy of the good. Here is a man, for instance, who is unwilling to join a local church. He's waiting until he finds a perfect church; and, of course, it will not be perfect anymore if he joins it. But he is a perfectionist, and he has such a concept of the ideal church that he is unwilling to work in a real church. His view of the invisible church makes him invisible at church. You see, the abstract best becomes the enemy of the concrete good.

I heard of a man who said to the preacher, "I want to sing in your choir."

The preacher replied, "But you don't belong here. Where do you have your membership?"

He said, "I don't belong to any local church. I belong to the invisible church."

The pastor said, "Then I suggest that you join the invisible choir."

Sometimes even preachers set their sights so high in the heavenlies that they are not worth much down in the earthlies. With them, people are either all good or all bad, and they are not able to work with people as they are.

Of course, people are either lost or saved. But most Christians are babes, and they are full of faults and flaws and imperfections. While they are saints in the sight of God, they are becoming saints in daily experience. We can be so demanding of God's sheep that we discourage them and drive them away. We sometimes set such a high standard that we become impatient with anything short of that standard. All the geese must be swans, and we expect all the rookies to act like veterans.

Our Lord worked with people as they were, and He was patient—not tolerant of sin, but compassionate. "A bruised reed shall he not break, and smoking flax shall he not quench" (Matthew 12:20). He was very merciful to frail humanity. The people that He did blast were the Pharisees, the religious hypocrites who thought they were the best.

We must not let the ideal best become the enemy of the actual good.

I don't suppose there is anyone quite so starry-eyed as a young preacher just out of school and in his first pastorate. What lofty dreams he has of a church where the deacons really "deak" and the choir never fusses, and where the committees do not spend their time keeping minutes and wasting hours.

But soon the honeymoon is over, and after a couple of ulcers he begins to take stock. He may find that the trouble is with him. Maybe the best has become the enemy of the good. Maybe he expected too much too soon, and he must learn to work with people as they are. This is not compromise. There is a blend of the ideal with the real and the heavenly with the earthly. While we do lament sometimes over how far short the best have fallen, we ought to rejoice in the bad that has become good, and in the good that has become better.

You see, a perfectionist has a pretty hard time of it. If he is a father, he thinks the children ought to be angels. If he is a choir director, all the singers ought to be prima donnas. If he is a Sunday school teacher, what on earth can make one want to hang his harp on the willows more than a dozen squirming little boys all over the bench with their feet where their heads ought to be. Yet twenty years later, he may learn that some of the seed took root in most unpromising soil.

I was under the pastorate of a great man of God, Dr. Clyde Turner, who for thirty-eight years was the pastor of the First Baptist Church of Greensboro. I remember his telling about a youngster in Sunday school who was a terror. Nobody knew what to do with him. Finally, he stopped coming. Dr. Turner said, "I am ashamed to say it, but I think we were all glad of it." Nobody made any special effort to get him back.

But one day they were having a little meeting and here came the boy running down the aisle with an instrument case under his arm. "Dr. Turner," he said, "they gave me a fiddle for being good."

"In the first place," said Dr. Turner, "I could imagine nobody giving him a fiddle; and in the second place, certainly not for being good.

The boy sensed the wonder on the pastor's countenance, and he said, "You see, doctor, I am gooder than I used to be."

Dr. Turner said, "I saw him scamper down the hall, and I

thought, 'Yes, thank God, by the grace of God a lot of us are 'gooder' than we used to be."

We have been sinners, and through no merit of our own and by no righteousness of our own we are "gooder" than we used to be because of what the Lord has done for us. You must deal patiently with people and take them as they are in the hope of that.

A long time ago I went to Moody Bible Institute as a student. I came fresh from the South, and I mean just that. I was from the South, and I was fresh. I played the piano a little, and I had an extra beat in it that I didn't even realize. I hadn't been there a week until some of the students started looking down their noses at me. One brother said, "Don't you know that syncopation has 'sin' in it?" Well, I didn't even know I was syncopating.

Then came that awful day when they said, "You must appear before the superintendent of men." I climbed the steps in fear and trembling. I could just visualize that man in there at his desk, and I could see him come down with his fist and say, "Keep your hands off that piano. We are not going to have this holy instrument desecrated around Moody Bible Institute."

I went in, and there was a mischievous twinkle in his eye as he said, "I knew when you came up from the South, brown-eyed and playing a piano, that we would have trouble." And then he gave me a nice Christian talk.

How do you suppose he wound it up? He said, "I want you to play tonight for the men's devotions." Oh, you ought to have seen me walk into that room that night with the superintendent of men, ready to play that piano. Napoleon never crossed the Alps with any more confidence than I had that night.

Now the superintendent was dealing with me as I was in the hope that I would become "gooder" than I used to be. If he had gone at it some other way, I probably would have added one more beat!

In personal experience we can become so demanding of ourselves that when we fail, we are almost overcome. We expect too much all of a sudden. We don't learn it all in a day. We do not grow up overnight. We ought to thank God for the progress already made and "onward urge our way."

Sometimes, we want to fly before we walk; we want to be perfect before we start toward perfection. Paul said, "I count not myself to have apprehended," but he also said, "By the grace of God I am what I am." He blended the ideal with the actual, and the best did not defeat the good.

It is not a mark of godliness to be forever condemning oneself in morbid self-accusation. Matthew Henry has a wonderful phrase about the "peaceable enjoyment of ourselves." We must not confuse obtainment with attainment. "Come unto me . . . and I will give you rest. Take my yoke upon you . . . and ye shall find rest" (Matthew 11:28-29).

Somebody wrote to a magazine editor and said, "Your magazine is not as good as it used to be."

He answered, "It never has been."

We sometimes feel that way about the good old days, but they also had their troubles. You must not lose sight of the ideal in the New Testament; but at the same time, God is working out His will through very weak saints who sometimes fall far short.

I often think of the salesman down our way who couldn't spell worth a nickel, but he certainly could sell. In the first letter he wrote back to his head office he said, "Boss, dis crowd that ain't never bought nothing of us, I've sold 'em $25,000 worth of goods."

Then he went on to Chicago and wrote back, "I've sold 'em $50,000 worth of goods."

The boss took those two letters, pinned them onto one of his own in which he purposely misspelled, and sent it to all the sales force. He said, "We have been spending too much time around here learning how to spell instead of how to sell. I want you to read these two letters and go and do like he dun."

D. L. Moody was not a scholarly man, but he recognized his own deficiencies. He sometimes wrote "dun," but, oh, what a bill of goods he sold for Almighty God. He used what he had and made it better to the glory of God.

Then there is the other truth about the good being the enemy of the best.

Our Lord said to the Pharisees, "Ye pay tithe of mint and anise and cummin, and have omitted the weightier matters of the law" (Matthew 23:23). You see, the good was getting in the way of the very best. The good is better than the bad, but we can become so occupied with the good that we miss the best.

I remember a meeting in a New York town many years ago where I used this old proverb. After the benediction I said to the song leader, a discerning young man, "Well, we had a good meeting tonight."

He said, "Too good."

"What do you mean?"

He said, "Do you know what you said in your sermon—that the good was the enemy of the best? I know this church; we ought to have been on our faces before God, but everybody settled for a good meeting."

Too many congregations are settling for a good meeting. It is harder to blast church members out of this state than it is to arouse sinners. A man who is living in gross iniquity may be shocked by the very enormity of his misdeeds to see his wretched state, but Laodiceans rich and increased with goods and needing nothing are the hardest people on earth to awaken.

You may be so busy with Bible conferences, evangelism, and converting bad people to become good people that you see no need for revival that converts good people into better people. As much as I want to see the bad become good, I believe we need a burden that the good shall have the best that God is providing.

The apostle Paul sets a goal in Philippians 3 that rebukes our complacency: "That I may know him, and the power of his resurrection, and the fellowship of his sufferings . . . forgetting those things which are behind," and that includes the bad, "and reaching forth unto those things which are before," and that includes the best. "I press toward the mark," not settling down in the good but moving through the actual to the ideal.

I would warn you about the peril of a lesser goal. Often what was merely meant to be the means becomes the end, and we arrive at our little goals and have no ambition to reach the main objective.

I asked a preacher, "How are you getting along?"

He said, "We are living in idolatry—just sitting around admiring our new church. We have arrived; we have it made— no more worlds to conquer."

What ought to be a milestone has become a millstone. We have run out of goals.

Preachers do that, too. They accumulate a few degrees, a trip to Palestine, a big car, a home in suburbia in a forest of television antennas. They have ecclesiastical security, financial security, social security, eternal security—all kinds of security. They have feathered their nests, they have everything, they have arrived. They've settled in the good, and they're not bothered about the best. They have settled like the Israelites in the promised land. Though there still remains much land to be possessed, they will never possess it. They are tired of fighting. From here on, they will rehash and reminisce and repeat. They have run out of goals. They have it made.

A preacher can do several things when he arrives at such a miserable state. First, he can resign. That is what Jeremiah wanted to do. He said, "I'm going to start a motel—get me a place out in the wilderness for traveling men" (Jeremiah 9:2). "I will testify to the tourists and give my money to good causes. I'm not going to work with this crooked generation anymore."

The preacher can quit. Some do their own resigning, and others are spared the trouble. Some spend five years resigning. Others leave overnight as though jet-propelled.

I don't find much information available on why preachers quit. You could stock a library with the reports of "the miracles that have happened here since I came." You would think Jonah was reporting on Nineveh. But I never read much on "why I went." Of course, we have these Cape Canaveral pastors who use their pulpits as a platform to blast off into a wider orbit.

Sometimes plain discouragement will do it. Anybody can quit. The church is full of quitters. You know that. They sang in the choir for a few weeks, and then their feelings were hurt, and the nightingale became a raven croaking, "Nevermore." Others come to church for months, and then golf becomes more important than God.

Preachers can quit, but resigning is not the way out.

Then you can *become* resigned. You can resign yourself to the status quo.

A preacher said to me, "I have decided that most of my church members are not going to be any better." Well, it would not take any special illumination to discover that generally over the country, but shall we accept it and ride along with it?

Another said to me, "I used to take a stand about dancing, and I just made enemies. I am going to go along with it." He did not mean that he was going to take up dancing. He had become resigned to the prevailing situation.

I'm glad Luther did not say, "I don't like the way things are going, but I'm not sticking my neck out." I'm glad Wesley didn't say, "I deplore the deadness of the age, but what can I do about it? I'm not risking my bread and butter."

You hear it everywhere today—that these things are here to stay. Of course they are! The devil is here to stay until the end of the age. Sin is here to stay. Liquor is here to stay. People are going to drink it, make it, and sell it; but that is no excuse for legalizing it. Immorality is here to stay, but that is no alibi for making it respectable. Television is here to stay. We don't expect to do away with all the television stations.

But then, that is no excuse to resigning oneself to letting the thing run wild.

Any Christian can get into a state where he is just resigned to the prevailing situation. You can avoid a lot of trouble and a lot of head-on collisions. But it's weakness to be resigned. What most of us need to be re-signed to our spiritual commission.

Let me ask you. How long has it been since you have re-signed? Is your commission like the old Declaration of Independence in the Archives Building? You cannot read it anymore? It has become faint? It needs re-signing. Any Christian can get into this state, and it was never any easier than it is now.

Dr. C. I. Scofield said that every time he and Mr. Moody prayed together, Moody would say, "God, renew Scofield's commission."

Dr. Scofield continued, "I got to worrying about that. Then I went to a meeting one night with a preacher friend. The sermon was on Naaman and his dipping in Jordan. It was a good sermon, but we had a feeling that something was lacking. My friend leaned over to me and said, 'What that brother needs is another dip in Jordan himself.' But it was not that brother that needed it. It was I. Out under the stars that night, I said, 'O Lord, I'm the one that needs a fresh dip in Jordan.'"

These days, we don't have many like Jabez saying, "Lord, I am not satisfied with my boundaries; widen my horizons and enlarge my coastline." (Too many comfortable saints today are expanding their physical waistline, but not enlarging their spiritual coastline.) Not many Calebs are saying, "Lord, I don't want to retire on a pension. Give me a mountain." Not many Pauls are saying, "I count not myself to have apprehended. I am not driving my tent pegs down in these lowlands; my prayer, my aim is higher ground."

If you are going to take the road to the best and not be satisfied with the good, you'll have a rough time of it. You'll be the target of the powers of darkness. You may be beset with strange maladies of body, mind, and spirit. You may be viewed with suspicion by your contemporaries, even in the church. You may be called a crank by the modernists for going too far, and you may be called a coward by the extremists for not going far enough. You may be a lonely man because, rather than settle down with Lot in Sodom, you insist on going on as a pilgrim with Abraham.

This road is not often traveled. Few there be that find the way to life, and fewer still who find the way to abundant life. A man who sets out to know Jesus Christ down here never arrives. He keeps on arriving all the time. He never fully apprehends, but he keeps on apprehending. He never knows Christ completely, but every day he knows Him better. That keeps him fresh. He is neither harsh nor bitter, because he expects nothing of himself, very little of others, and everything of God.

He is not satisfied with things as they are, but he is not impatient. He's not content with the good; but at the time, he enjoys the good. He doesn't confuse the end of the chapter with the end of the book. He doesn't settle for a lesser goal. Each experience is not a stopping place; it's a steppingstone. Each victory will help him win another. He may lose a battle now and then, but he wins the war.

Now, if you settle down snug in your smug complacency, God help you to set your sights on a better goal. Setting out to know God in Jesus Christ is the greatest of all pursuits in this world. It is an art—an art of the heart. The men who know God are never very plentiful, and they are not usually conspicuous; they do not make the headlines.

Many times, when I go to places for meetings, I am shown where the president of the bank lives. Sometimes I would like to see where the greatest saint lives, but I do not find out often. It might be on the other side of the railroad tracks.

I feel like saying, "I don't care where the president of the bank lives, but I would like to know where another president lives: 'He that ruleth his spirit is mightier than he that taketh a city.' Can you show me somebody who, by the grace of God, is the president over his own spirit?"

There are a lot of presidents today, president of this and that, who never rule their own spirits—as their wives can testify.

To know Christ and the power of His resurrection and the fellowship of His sufferings—that is the art of all arts and calls for devotion.

William Law used to say, "Who am I to lie folded up in a bed late of a morning when farmers have already gone about their work and I am so far behind with my sanctification?" Now we might disagree on sanctification if we started discussing it, but one thing we ought to agree on is that we are all behind with our sanctification.

The other day, rummaging through some old books, I came upon a newspaper clipping about a sermon I preached forty-five years ago in a little North Carolina town. I said to my wife, "I ought to be a better preacher, and I ought to be a better Christian as long as I have had to work at it."

Did you ever get bothered about that? What a sorry one you are after all the time you've had to read the Word of God, pray, and witness.

The difference between Paderewski and just anybody pounding a piano is more than genius. It is devotion and love for the art; it is time and toil. The difference between the man who knows God and an ordinary Christian is just that—devotion and love, time and toil. It takes time to be holy. Yes, it takes more than that, more than most of us are willing to give.

Really, one cannot be much of a television fan and get to know God very well. Jim Elliott, who was no octogenarian bewailing the evil times and longing for the good old days, said, "I went to my friend's house last night and looked at TV. God convicted me with Psalm 119:37: 'Turn away mine eyes from beholding vanity.' I sensed the powerful decentralizing effect of it on my mind and affections. It quickens me in ways not of God, defeating the purpose of prayer to be quickened in ways divine. Lord, grant me a disciplined spirit and an obedient body henceforth."

There was a red-blooded man out to know God, and he did in that short life he lived.

But, of course, knowing God is not a big item in the preparation of a lot of preachers over America today because, just between you and me, pulpit committees are not asking, "Does this prospective pastor know God?" They are asking, "Can he raise the budget?"

How the devil does fight the pursuit of God. Some of you will bear me witness that you never knew what satanic opposition was until you set out for a closer walk with God. Any housewife knows that the best way to remember the things she meant to do and forgot is to start praying. They will come to her mind to divert her from prayer. The devil will let a preacher prepare a sermon if it will keep him from preparing himself.

If some sour notes and discords are creeping in, let the Holy Spirit get a word in edgewise. He may say, "Stop staging concerts long enough to tune up your instrument."

If you are developing pockets of resentment and criticism of God's servants and of your people, the Holy Spirit might say, "Quit lecturing on health long enough to have a checkup yourself."

You see, we will settle for anything in this world short of knowing God. If the devil cannot sell you a bad bill of goods, then he will try to sell something good if it will be a substitute. Even church work can crowd out God. Pastors become not undershepherds of a flock, but heads of a department store.

The only way to break out of this trap is to become a rebel in the rat race and make time for God at any cost. If you cannot untie knots, cut them. Learn how to say a great big healthy "No!" Cancel that engagement to speak for the sons and daughters of "I Will Arise" and tell them, "I have an appointment." You do—with God.

George B. Duncan, in one of his Keswick messages, said, "I

have a date with my boys just like I have an appointment with anyone else; and when something tries to break in on that, I say I have an appointment." How much more important it is to keep an appointment with the Almighty.

One year, I took off most of May and June just to be still and try to read and pray and think. Now, I am not on a salary, and my income stops when I stop. But there is another income; and if you don't get that, then no other income is going to matter. I wasn't sick. I could have had plenty of preaching to do. I could have gone to Europe. But sometimes it is more of a distinction to stay home.

How about your other income, my preacher friend? The real depression is not when the stock market crashes; it is when your income stops—the unconscious bankruptcy of Laodicea. We're rich and increased with goods, and we don't know that we are broke.

The tax forms have a place for "other income," but so far the tax collector has found no way to put a levy on my other income. If you are going to have a heavenly income, however, you have to give time to that investment.

Years ago, I was with Dr. Paul Rees at his conference at Medicine Lake. I remember a wonderful illustration that he told of a bishop in India who was approached by a missionary. She said, "Bishop, I have sought a deeper experience with God all these years and I don't have it. I have read books. I have read what to do and all the rules, but I am nowhere yet. Does God have favorites?"

The old bishop said, "No, my dear, God does not have favorites. But He has intimates."

Most men are strangers to God today. Some are acquainted with Him, but only a few are intimates—those who have made it their business to know Him. Forgetting the bad behind them, they press through the good around them to reach the best before them; and for that they are predestined to be conformed to the image of His Son.

My pastor used a good illustration the other night. He said

there was a young art student whose teacher put him to painting a sunset. He sat on the brow of a hill, looking across, trying to capture on canvas the glory that filled the west. But he spent too much time working on one detail. The old teacher came along and said, "Look, the sun is almost down, and you are spending your time putting a roof on a barn."

The application is clear for all of us. The sun is going down. "Fast to its close ebbs out life's little day." What a tragedy to shingle a barn and miss the sunset—to let the bad or even the good keep us from the best. There is nothing wrong with painting the barn, but everything is wrong if it makes you miss painting the sunset.

God save you from stopping at any lesser goal than to know Him, and the power of His resurrection, and the fellowship of His sufferings, being made conformable unto His death.

## WAKE UP AND GET UP

Not since Manhattan Island was sold for $24 has there been so much dirt available for so little money as now.

# Wake Up and Get Up

*And that, knowing the time, that now it is high time to awake out of sleep: for now is our salvation nearer than when we believed. The night is far spent, the day is at hand: let us therefore cast off the works of darkness, and let us put on the armor of light. Let us walk honestly, as in the day; not in rioting and drunkenness, not in chambering and wantonness, not in strife and envying. But put ye on the Lord Jesus Christ, and make not provision for the flesh, to fulfill the lust thereof* (Romans 13:11-14).

Jeremiah broke just about all the rules for successful preaching, but he knew what God had to say to his generation. The false prophets of his time were preaching serenity and peace of mind, saying, "Peace, peace, when there is no peace; peace and safety, peace and security," when sudden destruction hung over their heads. But Jeremiah was not a tranquilizer.

I've often wondered what a psychiatrist would have said if he had checked the prophet. He would have said he was too pessimistic, had the war jitters, should take a rest in Florida, was antisocial, not a good mixer, too interested in prophecy, not good for public morale.

While the happiness boys were spreading cold cream on cancers, dusting off sin with a feather duster, and singing, "Brighten the corner where you are," Jeremiah was saying, "Get out of the corner where you are. Judgment is upon us!"

None of the experts of his time had any use for Jeremiah. The feeling was mutual. He called the prophet Hananiah a liar. But in the hour of extremity, Zedekiah, the king, turned to the prophet in prison. We are coming to a day when the prophet who knows what God is saying may well have to tell it from jail.

In the New Testament, Paul in a Roman prison understood the times better than all the wise men in the empire. He pictured our day as "perilous." If you put together what Paul said, what our Lord said, and what all the New Testament says, you have a picture that is as up-to-date as today's paper. It is summed up in three words: anarchy, apostasy, and apathy.

Organized anarchy and Communism control more people after sixty years than Christianity after two thousand. We made our first blunder when we recognized anarchy as though it were decent government. We made it respectable. We have sat at tables with international gangsters as though they were gentlemen. You might as well call a conference of the underworld to discuss law and order. Criminals can't establish justice. A truce with the devil won't guarantee righteousness.

We are being deceived by friendly gestures today, forgetting that a bear can hug you to death. Some time ago, I read of a bear that was out looking for his breakfast and a hunter who was out looking for a fur coat. They had a summit conference; the bear had his breakfast, and the hunter was inside his fur coat.

Anarchy terrorizes our communities now as teenage gangsters murder for fun and law enforcement is at its wit's end. Anarchy has made a shambles of many homes and orphans of many children. Anarchy fills the bookracks with literature too filthy for the gutter, and even the courts defend it.

I was riding along a highway the other day and saw a sign, "Dirt for sale." I said, "They ought to hang that over every rack on paper-bound books in the drugstores of America." Not since Manhattan Island was sold for $24 has there been so much dirt available for so little money as now.

Anarchy blasts the eardrums with the discords of the jungle today; but I shouldn't even call it jungle, out of respect for the apes that must be ashamed of it.

Anarchy makes the heart a rebel, deceitful, and desperately wicked.

Not only is there anarchy, but there is apostasy—a falling away from the faith, a turning from truth to fables. Men cannot endure sound doctrine. False teachers abound. Let no one deceive you into thinking, because of the current interest in religion, that unbelief no longer besets the church. If modernism and liberalism are dead, their ghosts haunt us more than ever; and if the demon of false doctrine has gone out the door, seven more have returned through the window.

A businessman who was accustomed to presiding at business functions was called upon suddenly to officiate at a church affair. He was used to the normal procedures of a business gathering when the minutes were read and he would move their adoption or approval. Somebody read the Scriptures, and this man absent-mindedly got up and said, "If there are no corrections, the Scriptures will stand as read."

Well, they will stand as read, and it is high time that we let them. The new unbeliefs speak the language of faith, but the devil does more harm as an angel of light than he ever accomplishes as a roaring lion. He thrives in the climate of consent when tolerance is exalted above the truth.

This falling away today, however, is not only from doctrine; it is also from the New Testament standard of Christian conduct. One does not have to be decent to be a church member. Church rolls are stuffed with multitudes of the unregenerate going to hell on a church letter. Others are saved, but they are noun Christians when they need to be adjective Christians. Don't forget that the word *Christian* is both a noun and an adjective. We need more Christian Christians.

We need to be careful how we say that orthodoxy is not the test of a Christian, or that the Christian life is not a matter, for instance, of to dance or not to dance, to drink or not to drink. Of course, those things are not the standard; but it is easy to give the impression that those things don't make much difference. This poor generation does not need any further encouragement to careless living.

This is a day of apostasy in creed, conduct, doctrine, and duty. The man who ignores it or minimizes it becomes a party to it. It is not enough to preach love. They had love in Thyatira, but Revelation 2:20 tells you that Jezebel put over her program just the same. If love alone will take care of everything, why didn't Paul begin his letter to the Corinthians with the thirteenth chapter?

Anarchy in the world, apostasy in the professing church, and in the true church, apathy—listlessness, indifference, smug complacency, resting at ease in Zion, lukewarmness—"neither cold or hot." The tragedy of this hour is that we are all mixed up living at a neither/nor position, when with God it is either/or. You see that everywhere in the international realm; we are neither at war nor at peace. You see it in the mixture of the church and the world—the church becoming worldly, the world becoming churchy. You see it in our strange effort to mix the old nature with the new.

During the First World War, Teddy Roosevelt thundered out against what he called hyphenated Americans, people who had a divided loyalty. He said, "America is not a polyglot boarding house. If you are an American and something else, you are not an American." By the same token, one could say today that if you are a Christian and something else, you are not a loyal Christian. There isn't any such thing as a 50 percent, 60 percent, 75 percent loyalty. A husband who is 85 percent loyal to his wife is not loyal at all.

God thundered against the people in Ezekiel's day who came to church: "Thou son of man, the children of thy people still are talking against thee by the walls and in the doors of the houses, and speak one to another, every one to his brother, saying, Come, I pray you, and hear what is the word that cometh forth from the Lord. And they come unto thee as the people cometh, and they sit before thee as my people, and they hear thy words, but they will not do them" (Ezekiel 33:30-31).

Isn't that a pretty good description of our situation today? We come, we sit—and how we can sit! James and John asked the Lord, "Grant that we may sit." That is all a lot of saints want to do here and hereafter—just sit. There has never been more superficial interest in religion than there is now. We're living at a comfortable seventy-two degrees, and the Lord of the lampstands is saying, "Be boiling and repent."

God's Word says, "Wake up and get up!" How do you get up in the morning? Not by merely thinking about it. If you lie there and think about it, you will probably go back to sleep and dream that you are awake, and then wake up and find out that you have been asleep.

How do you get up? By feeling like it? No. You either get up or you don't. A lot of our activity often mistaken for revival is just the church turning over, but not waking up. Turning over is not getting up, and waking up is not getting up. The Word of God says we're to get up and go about our business for the king.

The only answer to anarchy and apostasy is Christ's appearing; and the only answer to apathy, if the Lord tarries, is an awakening. "We are not of the night, nor of darkness. Therefore let us not sleep, as do others; but let us watch and be sober" (1 Thessalonians 5:5-6).

"Let us never fall into the sleep that stupefies the rest of the world," says the Phillips translation. "It is high time to awake out of sleep." "Awake to righteousness, and sin not; for some have not the knowledge of God: I speak this to your shame" (1 Corinthians 15:34).

The other day the Episcopalians installed a bishop coadjutor in one of their areas. Down my way a radio announcer tried to tell us about it, but he had never seen that word before. He said, "So-and-so has been installed as bishop co-agitator." We need a bishop co-agitator today in partnership with God, agitating the people.

Some say we need another Amos. Well, we do, but did you ever try being one at the First Church Bethel on Sunday morning at 11:00 A.M.? It is easier to build monuments to the prophets than it is to copy them. "Seven towns contend for Homer dead, through which the living Homer begged his bread."

Joseph Parker said, "We clap our hands applaudingly at the name of Bunyan, but many would not admit a living Bunyan into fellowship. They might give him something at the back door." It is one thing to applaud the heroes and the prophets and the seers; it is another thing to recognize the succession today.

The tragedy of the hour is that the situation is desperate, but the saints are not. If they were, we would have revival. But, as in the days of Jeremiah, we have too many lullaby crooners and not enough prophets.

Wouldn't you think that in an hour like this the churches would be filled with penitent worshipers, praying even all night while there is time? Why are saints so anxious to get their sleep, while sinners revel all night? Come to think of it, most church members stay up after all, feasting their eyes on Sodom and Gomorrah brought into their living rooms.

Some of the churches down my way are putting in glass fronts. You can walk along the street and see what's going on in church. It's a bad time for glass fronts, though; not enough is going on inside.

Consider the way the average church in America observes New Year's Eve. At 7:30, a picture; then games; followed, of course, by refreshments. (I used to say "as poor as a church mouse." I stopped saying that. I don't know of anything getting fatter than a church mouse these days.) Then along about quarter to 12:00, they have a little devotional. With judgment overhead, you would think there would be a prayer meeting. But there wouldn't be any use in trying to put one on with a majority of the people more willing to play than to pray. They're in no mood for prayer. And yet, what kind of Christians are we that we don't want that kind of meeting?

God has said, "If My people will . . . then I will . . ." But who wants to humble himself, to pray and seek God's face, and turn from his wicked ways? What would happen if in our great denominational convocations we would throw the printed program into the wastebasket and go to our knees in desperate prayer? "Ah," somebody says, "but we don't come to these places for revival. We come to attend to business." What greater business do we have than to seek a divine visitation?

I'm not preaching alarmism. I'm not disturbed by evil tidings. My heart is fixed, trusting in the Lord.

Dr. Carter Helm Jones tells about his daddy who lost everything he had in the Civil War. One morning he and the faithful old servant on the place had to make a long trip. They arose long before day and started off in the old hack. Dr. Jones fell asleep in the back, but after a while he was rudely awakened. The carriage had come to a stop, and the old driver was out by the side of the road on his knees praying.

Dr. Jones said, "What's the matter, Mose?"

"Oh," he said, "boss, get down here and pray. The judgment day has come!"

Dr. Jones said later, "I took in the situation immediately. There was a meteoric shower, and it did look as if judgment day had come for, as we say, the stars were falling. I got out and knelt beside the old driver and said, 'Look, Mose, do you see that star over yonder?' And I pointed to the morning star.

"He said, 'Yes.'

"Then I said, 'Let's get back into the hack and resume our journey. I'm going back to sleep, and you keep your eyes on that star. If *it* falls, then you wake me up.'"

Oh, we are living in a meteoric shower—the stars are falling (movie stars, athletic stars, political stars, TV stars) all the way from hero to zero in ten minutes these days. I saw a new book in our library the other day right beside *Who's Who*. It is called *Who Was Who*.

Don't let these man-made satellites and dogs in space and monkeys in orbit upset you too much. Get your eyes on another Star. "The kings of the earth set themselves, and the rulers take counsel together, against the Lord, and against his anointed" (Psalm 2:2). Keep your eyes on that Star.

We are not of the night and of the darkness; we know what time it is. But I wonder if the only weapon, the only effective weapon left the church now, is not desperate prayer. Maybe we are too far gone for anything else. It is time to give up halfway measures.

I get so weary of announcing "services as usual." That's the trouble. They ought to be unusual—everything else is. We are trying to meet short-term emergencies with long-range programs. It's too late.

Lyndon Johnson said once, "It is up to all Americans to work as though there would never be a tomorrow and as though everything must be done today." It is time the church developed an urgency born out of the pressures of this fantastic hour. Politicians don't know what time it is; but we know. Because we know, our responsibility is great.

Remember Daniel. God gave him the blueprints of all time to come. After those fearful revelations and that double vision of Antiochus Epiphanes and Antichrist in chapter eight, what did Daniel do? Did he strut around and say, "You Chaldeans don't know what time it is, but I know. I've got the inside track"? No. He humbled himself in one of the greatest prayers of confession in the Word of God.

Mr. Moody said, "If you go back to the Scripture records, you will find that the men who lived nearest to God were those who confessed their sins and failures."

Daniel confessed his sins and those of his people, and yet there is nothing recorded against Daniel. He was one of the best men on the face of the earth, but his confession of sin was one of the deepest. Daniel confessed first that "we have sinned"; second, we "have committed iniquity"; third, we "have done wickedly"; fourth, we "have rebelled" against Thee; fifth, we have departed "from Thy precepts" (Daniel 9:5). Daniel was humbling himself before God as the worst of sinners.

We Bible Christians have no business becoming complacent. It is a long time since I've heard about getting low in the dust and confessing our unworthiness, our sinfulness, and our utter dependence on God.

I wonder what D. L. Moody would say. He might say something he said a long time ago that some people wouldn't like: "I firmly believe that the church of God will have to confess her own sins before there can be any great work of grace. I sometimes think it is time to give up preaching to the ungodly and preach to those who profess to be Christians." Think of that!

Our Lord said, "He that hath an ear, let him hear what the Spirit saith to the churches"—the churches, not the church. The church is the building, the Body, and the Bride; but here it is the local "churches." There is a lot of preaching about the church today that doesn't consider the church on the corner. There is no such thing as revival in general apart from the local church. The man who is best qualified to judge whether we're having revival or not is not the scholar, nor the evangelist; it's the pastor of the local church. Any revival worth talking about will show up in the local assembly, because it is the thermometer of the spiritual climate any time.

For years I have gone up and down this land—one week, one church—week after week after week. I don't stand on the outside of the church and knock it. I try to stand on the inside and exhort it. I do not agree with those who say that God is bypassing the local churches today, that He is in too big a hurry to plod along with our local assemblies, that He is using other movements to get the job done more quickly. God does use the irregular, but only to feed back into the regular. God's program will never bypass the local church. "He that hath an ear, let him hear what the Spirit saith unto the churches."

We shall never have moving revival until we acknowledge the sovereignty of the Spirit of God. Like Ahab and Jehoshaphat, we draw up our plans and ask God to bless them, when we should be asking God for the plans. We decide what kind of service we want at 11:00 A.M., or what kind of revival we want. And then we're disappointed if we don't have it. We need to let God give us His pattern from the holy mount. We write the score and expect the Holy Spirit to play it. We plot the course and expect the Holy Spirit to follow it. We expect God to sign on our dotted line. God is not signing on anybody's little dotted line.

How long will it take us to get to the point where we acknowledge His total authority? Are we so in love with our plans that we are unwilling to bow to the Holy Spirit? Would you be willing to throw away all your plans? Would your organization be willing to throw away all its plans if the Holy Spirit has better ones? Would you be willing for the next revival to start with another denomination? Would you be willing for it to start in your town in the little church across the railroad tracks? Would you be willing for it to start with some other race, some other nation?

This thing comes and sits on our own doorsteps. Have I ever bowed to the absolute sovereignty of the Holy Spirit? Do I lie to Him, grieve Him, quench Him? Do I regard my body as His temple? Have I ever been filled with the Holy Spirit? Or would I rather miss a blessing than to give up a prejudice? The trouble with us today is that we say we are depending on the Holy Spirit; but we are actually so wired up with our own devices that if the fire does not fall from heaven, we can turn on a switch and produce false fire of our own. If there is no sound of a mighty rushing wind, our furnace is all set to blow hot air instead. God save us from a synthetic Pentecost!

The Lord said, "Without me ye can do nothing." Well, that all depends upon what you mean by "nothing." The trouble is, we can do a lot of things without Him. We can preach, prophesy, do wonderful works, build churches, add members, raise money, be the biggest thing in town, without the Holy Spirit's being anywhere near the place. But we can do nothing acceptable or pleasing in His sight. All is vain unless the Spirit of the Holy One comes down.

Eight times in the gospels we read, "He that hath ears to hear, let him hear." Eight times in Revelation we read, "He that hath an ear, let him hear." To Laodicea, He said, "If any man hear my voice." Have you noticed how broad that verse is? It really says, "If anyone hear my voice, anybody in the whole church"; but it is as narrow as the one who hears His voice and opens the door.

He is not waiting for a committee to pass a resolution; He is waiting for somebody, anybody, to open the door—somebody with an ear for God. We study how to talk, but we need to learn how to listen. After all, God gave us two ears to hear with and only one mouth to talk with—thank the Lord! We have ears; but hearing, we hear not.

Many years ago, I was at a centennial gathering and heard some things that I have never forgotten. One of the speakers was Dr. V. Raymond Edman, who said, "I used to go to the old Bible conferences and at the end of a message I didn't want to speak to anybody. I wanted to go home and pray. Now we go out and say, 'How did you like the speaker?'" The preaching of the Word should send us to our homes in no mood for trivial conversation, but ready to do business with God.

Rummaging through my father's papers the other day, I came across this old well-worn statement: "Nothing is ever settled till it is settled right, and nothing is ever settled right till it is settled with God." God invites us to talk it over: "Come now, and let us reason together" (Isaiah 1:18). Job said, "Surely I would speak to the Almighty, and I desire to reason with God" (Job 13:3). He had lost out in the lower courts, and he had prepared his brief. He said, "I'm appealing to the highest tribunal."

We have never had as many unsettled problems as we have now.

*World peace.* Practically all the reforms and movements now underfoot, all the things that we are trying to put over these days, are not the birth pangs of a new order; they are the dying gasps of civilization. The carcass is nearly ready for the vultures. He is a poor spiritual bird-watcher who doesn't know the difference between the dove of peace and the vulture of judgment.

*Home problems.* Never were so many homes on the rocks and more of them almost there. Some of them get patched up, and they hold together for decency's sake. Domestic problems will never be settled until they are settled with God.

*Church problems.* I'm thinking now of a church that has just called a new preacher. The people have an idea that a new preacher is the panacea for all their ills. They have never got right with God and with their last preacher. They have never apologized; they have never repented for the way they have treated their last pastor. They cannot let bygones be bygones, for God doesn't deal that way. There will never be spiritual health in that organism until the pus pockets of iniquity are lanced and drained and cleansed.

*Personal problems.* I think of a young fellow who was called to preach, and he turned God down. Now he is making money, but he is drinking and his home is threatened. He says, "I'm going to straighten up. I'm going to quit this habit. I'm going to join the church. I'm going to settle it." No, he won't, not that way. Seven demons return after a housecleaning like that, and the last state of that man will be worse than the first because nothing is ever settled right until it is settled with God.

Among God's people, there are enough unsettled problems to fill an encyclopedia if they were listed. What is yours? A personal habit over which you have no victory? Trouble in your home that you wouldn't have anybody outside know about, because you're a church worker and both of you claim to be Christians? You are a youngster and claim to be a Christian, yet you do not honor your father and mother? You have a problem of guidance, a difficulty between you and someone else, a church problem?

Any Christian who cannot get enough grace from God to solve his own problems is not ready to tell everybody else how to settle theirs. Any two Christians who cannot somehow have a session with God and settle their problem are not ready to say that Christ is the answer to somebody else's problem. Any church that cannot lay hold of enough of the grace of God to settle its own difficulties has no business telling about a cure that hasn't been tried at home.

If you have a problem that hasn't been settled, will you be humble enough and honest enough to acknowledge it—a problem in your heart, in your home, in your church? Maybe you are a preacher with a great load. Settle your problem. Settle it right. Settle it with God.

The only answer to anarchy and apostasy is Christ's appearing; the only answer to apathy is an awakening.

## ALAS!

We're doing everything today but dealing with sin in the church. We dare not touch it with a forty-foot pole. Achan gets away with the wedge of gold, and the Ananias and Sapphira club is not rebuked.

# Alas!

The little word *alas*—an exclamation as well as an expression of disappointment, sorrow, and woe—is found many times in Scripture, but the first one is found in Joshua 7. The invasion of Canaan had just begun, and God's people suffered a severe setback at Ai. Joshua fell on his face and said, "Alas, O Lord GOD, wherefore hast thou at all brought this people over Jordan, to deliver us into the hand of the Amorites, to destroy us? would to God we had been content, and dwelt on the other side Jordan!" (Joshua 7:7). We might call this "the alas of a defeated church."

We've been put to shame, and the pagans go by asking, "Where is now your God?" The answer is not to be found in lamenting that we ever crossed over Jordan. The answer is to be found in the word of our Lord. God said to him, "Get up. This is no time for a prayer meeting. There's sin in the camp that must be dealt with." And even though just one man may be involved, the transgression involves the entire corporate body. Victory followed when they dealt with Achan.

Then Joshua said in verse 13, "Up, sanctify the people, and say, Sanctify yourselves against tomorrow." This repeats the command of Joshua 3:5. We need to do a lot of sanctifying of ourselves against tomorrow. Although we don't know what tomorrow will bring, we do know what some tomorrows are going to bring—death and judgment.

We're doing everything today but dealing with sin in the church. We dare not touch it with a forty-foot pole. Achan gets away with the wedge of gold, and the Ananias and Sapphira club is not rebuked. The stone is not rolled away from before the sepulcher because it might create, as Martha suggested, an unpleasant situation. God hasn't called us to raise Lazarus; He will do that. He has called us to roll away the stone. He won't do the supernatural thing until we do the simple thing. We try to do what only God can do, and we don't do what we must do.

Some pastors say, "Well, I don't want to preach against sin in my church because it might dig up more snakes than I could kill." You don't need to be afraid of that. But there won't be any victory until sin is exposed and the sinners are brought to repentance.

Now Joshua could have said, as I hear some of our church leaders saying today, "Oh, let's forget our differences and regroup our forces. Let's square our shoulders and march ahead. Then everything will come out all right." It wouldn't have come out right at Ai. They would have marched to another defeat. We step up the program of the churches today, and one defeat follows another—and will, until we do what is indicated here.

There are four *A*'s in Joshua 7. There's *Ai*—and may I ask you, do you have an Ai in your life, a place of defeat where the Canaanites have gotten the better of you? Then there's an *alas,* the alas of desperation. Have you come to that point? Because, if you have, there's some hope for you. Then there's an *Achan* in this chapter; he's the essential trouble. Have you dealt with *Achan*—the essential source of trouble—in your life?

When they did deal with Achan, they did it in the valley of *Achor,* the place of confrontation where you face up to what's wrong and do something about it. And don't forget that Hosea 2:15 says the valley of Achor shall be a door of hope. I believe the door of hope for the church today lies in the valley of Achor, where, after the defeat at Ai, we cry to God with the alas of desperation and get up and do something about it.

The second "alas" is found in 1 Kings 13. God, when sending His messenger to rebuke Jeroboam, had told him, "Now don't accept any hospitality in Bethel. Come back home."

He started off very well. He warned the king and started

home. But an old prophet overtook him and prevailed upon him to come back and eat dinner. So the prophet who had turned down an invitation from the king let another prophet deceive him. As a result, he was overtaken by a lion, and the last thing we read in that story is really the epitaph on his grave: "Alas, my brother!" We don't even know his name.

This strange story has always fascinated me. Every once in a while I get out Alexander Whyte's sermon on it. It frightens me everytime I read it, but I do it for my edification.

Why did this prophet collapse when he was just about to become one of the greatest spokesmen in the Old Testament? Was he just tired? He had confronted a king—the arch apostate of the time—and had brought him to his knees. His conscience was clear, his stomach was empty, and his nerves were on edge. That makes a bad combination.

He got under the tree and said, "Well, perhaps I should have had dinner with the king. Maybe I am following too austere a policy here. Maybe I should let my hair down."

You know, the prophets never fared very well in the shade. Elijah had trouble under the juniper and Jonah under the gourd vine. This one decided to go back for dinner with that other prophet.

Alexander Whyte says to preachers, "Your people will not care one straw what you say from the pulpit if you sup heartily with them afterward." John Bunyan said that many a sermon is lost in the Sunday dinner. G. Campbell Morgan spoke about more prophets being ruined by eating out than in any other way.

Robert Murray McCheyne warned of the danger of a preacher's being too much a lover of good eating; and Charles G. Finney said, "Do not make the impression that you're fond of good dinners and like to be invited out to dine. It'll be a snare to you and a stumbling block to them." Now that's something you haven't heard in a long time. Many a revival begins with a solemn message and dies when the preacher gets in the home to laugh and talk it away in a round of hilarity.

I used to think of the preachers in my boyhood days as stern, and they were. But I prefer them still to the hale-fellow-well-met who starts out to be the life of the party and finds out it is the death of the prophet. When a pastor gets to the place that his parishioners call him by his first name, he's in trouble. He's not supposed to be "one of them"; he's supposed to be ahead of them. The preacher who jests and jokes too much cannot stand on Sunday and reprove and rebuke and exhort.

I am sure that when this Bethelite prophet and his son got this preacher into their home for dinner, they were a bit awed at first because here was a man who had started a revival. God was with him. But as they ate and laughed and talked, the prophet of God lost his dignity and became as one of them. Beware of those Bethelites who are not grieved for the affliction of Joseph. Beware of hobnobbing with those that rest at ease in Zion. Don't get too chummy with Sodom and Gomorrah.

This disobedient prophet not only lost his life, but the revival went on the rocks and Jeroboam reverted to his old ways. Nothing confirms evil men in their course more than the backsliding of the righteous. Beloved, you and I are under serious orders; and many a preacher's tombstone might well bear the lament, "Alas, my brother!"

I remember a certain preacher who started out so gloriously and ended up under a cloud. Another minister said of him, "There was a day when he was my greatest inspiration, but there came a day when he was my greatest warning."

The "alas of the disobedient prophet" should be a great warning to us. We're not going to see another revival until the ministry recovers its solemn commission and learns to say no to Jeroboam and all the priests of Bethel. They will offer rewards to break down any preacher whose old-fashioned devotion to duty makes him a poor mixer. He makes them uncomfortable by contrast, and they want to reduce the disparity by clever devices so innocent in appearance that he appears ungracious if he declines their favors.

The third "alas" is found in 2 Kings 6:1-7. It is the "alas of departed power." Many men have preached from it—the lost axhead.

There's a lot of wood chopping going on today, but the chips are few; the results, meager. These young sons of the prophets took off on a wood-chopping expedition to the Jordan River. But the axhead flew off one young man's handle and landed in the water. He cried out, "Alas, master! for it was borrowed."

Elisha's young prophet was concerned, and I do thank the Lord that he quit chopping. There are some today who keep on chopping after the axhead is gone—at least, they go through the motions. They grab a substitute, labor in the energy of the flesh, and pound because they can't expound. Somebody said, "There's an abundance of energy in the church today, but it's not conquering energy conscious of its power. It's feverish energy concious of its powerlessness."

But you say, "My church work has to go on some way, even if we can't do it the right way. The budget has to be met. The expenses have to be paid." Beloved, God's work must be done by God's people in God's way; and if it isn't done that way, you might as well not do it at all.

When the young prophet was asked where the axhead fell, he knew. The place to get back in God's will is the place where you got out. Have you ever shown God the place? He knows where it is, but have you ever dealt specifically with where you lost the power? "He that covereth his sins shall not prosper: but whoso confesseth and forsaketh them shall have mercy" (Proverbs 28:13).

Then, thank God, the iron did swim. God restores lost power. He is the God of another chance—not hereafter, but now. Jacob and Samson and David and Jonah and Peter all had another try.

Why does the Holy Spirit go to all the trouble of saying, "And he put out his hand and took it"? Why all that extra information? James tells us that when we need wisdom, we are to pray for it and then believe we've got it. We're to put out our hands, as it were, and take it. We lie to God in prayer if we don't rely on God after prayer. Mark 11:24 says, "What things soever ye desire, when ye pray, believe that ye receive them, and ye shall have them."

That is strange grammar. Believe you've got it, and you will get it. Well, that's the way it is. Don't worry about the grammar. Do what God says. When you ask for restored power, take it by faith if you have dealt with the trouble first.

Also in 2 Kings 6 there is another "alas" in the life of Elisha. This is the "alas of desperate crisis."

My, Elisha was a good man to have around. He was equal to any emergency. If the food was poisoned, he made it fit to eat. If the water was bitter, he made it sweet. He could recover lost axheads, and he could put a widow in the oil business at a good profit. He was a mighty man. Naaman came to him with his troubles, and the king sought his counsel. He was never at a loss to know what to do, no matter how trivial or tremendous the issue.

The king of Syria sent an army after him. Elisha's servant went out on the back porch and looked and saw soldiers everywhere. He ran back in and said, "Alas, my master! What shall we do?"

But old Elisha wasn't disturbed. Neither lost axheads nor lost armies upset his equilibrium. He came out and looked too, but he didn't bother looking down. He looked up, and there were angels everywhere, because the angels of the Lord encamp around about them that fear Him to deliver them. He said, "Lord, open this fellow's eyes so he can see."

Ephesians 6:12 in one of the newer translations goes like this in part, "We are up against the unseen power that controls this dark world, and spiritual agents from the very headquarters of evil."* The devil has mobilized his reserve for a fight to the finish, and we ought not underestimate our adversaries. That's a great mistake militarily and spiritually.

*J. B. Phillips, *New Testament in Modern English.*

Teddy Roosevelt had a little dog that was always getting in fights and always getting licked.

Somebody said, "Colonel, he's not much of a fighter."

The colonel replied, "Oh, yes, he's a good fighter. He's just a poor judge of dogs."

It's a good thing to know what we are up against, but we're too inclined to count our adversaries and discount our allies. Oh, how we need to list our assets instead of bemoaning our liabilities. The saints of the past were on our side. The saints of today are on our side. The angels are on our side. And best of all, God is with us.

I was in a small southern town where there was a little repair shop run by a fellow named Angel. He had a sign in the window: Angel Service.

I said, "Why, I've had that all my life." Are they not all ministering spirits?

I think of that glorious hour when Paul took stock of his adversaries in Romans 8. He made a wide sweep and took in the visible and the invisible on earth and in heaven. He included tribulation, persecution, distress, famine, peril, and sword. You'd have thought that would be enough, but he was just getting started. He took in death and life and rose up to include angels and principalities and powers. Then he came down to earth for things present and dipped into the future for things to come. He went up for heights and down for depths; and to make sure he hadn't overlooked anything, he added, "Any other creature."

That's taking in the territory, friend. Oh, what a formidable aggregation. But he declares that the whole combination cannot separate us from the love of God, and that's just another way of saying, "Fear not: for they that be with us are more than they that be with them."

It's time we stopped groaning over our adversaries and started glorying in our allies. The battle is the Lord's. The victory is already won. Our Waterloo is behind us. Even the statistics we gloomily quote so much are on our side and in our favor. I agree with the old Scotsman who said, "Whoever heard of anybody ever drowning with his head that high above water?" There's nothing to fear if you believe the Word of God.

Elisha prayed, "Lord, open his eyes." Jesus healed at least three blind people. One he just touched, and another he touched twice, and another he sent to the pool of Siloam. I can imagine those fellows getting together later and discussing it.

One said to another, "I see you got your sight. How did it happen?"

He said, "Well, the Master touched me just once."

And if the second were like some Christians I know, he would have said, "That's not the orthodox way. You've got to be touched twice."

And the third one said, "You're both wrong. You've got to put mud on your eyes and go wash it off in the pool of Siloam."

They would have started two new denominations right there—the Mudites and the Anti-mudites. Oh, I don't care how it happened, friend. It happened. It's no time for an "alas." It's time for an "alleluia."

That's exactly what you find in Revelation 18 and 19. Chapter 18 is full of "alases." Notice verse 10 is all about Babylon: "Alas, alas, that great city Babylon, that mighty city!" In verse 16 we have, "Alas, alas, that great city." In verse 19 we have, "Alas, alas, that great city." But when you get over to chapter 19, they switch from "alas" to "alleluia." It's "alleluia" in verse 1, and it's "alleluia" in verse 3 and verse 4 and verse 6. Have you ever made the switch, friend, from "alas" to "alleluia?"

Bible scholars have argued about Babylon, and I don't have time to go into it. I don't personally think it is the old metropolis of antiquity restored. Is it Rome that Peter called Babylon? Was that a code name? I believe it's part of the last world's political and ecclesiastical confederacy under Antichrist, and it's shaping up now in the world church before our very eyes. A lot of good people think they're building the New Jerusalem when they're just building old Babylon.

I read in chapter 18:2 that it's for the birds—"a cage of every unclean and hateful bird." Friend, I'm not building for the birds today. All Christians belong to the holy nation, the heavenly kingdom in this world; but when the professing church starts working with this world to create the kingdom of heaven out of the devices of men, we're in the wrong business. We become part of the Babylon that we are told to come out of.

Oh, you'll be despised and persecuted if you're going to be a stranger in Babylon today. But I'm not affiliated with the movement that ends in "alas." And that's what this world order is going to end up with—"alas."

But thank God, I'm lined up in a cause that ends in an "alleluia," the alleluia of the victorious Christ, the rider on the white horse!

# THE MAN GOD USES

It is one of the ironies of the ministry that the very man who works in God's name is often hardest put to find time for God. The parents of Jesus lost Him at church, and they were not the last ones to lose Him there.

# The Man God Uses

God is on the lookout today for a man who will be quiet enough to get a message from Him, brave enough to preach it, and honest enough to live it.

The man God uses must be still and know that He is God. We live in a world hysterical with moral and spiritual delirium tremens. The human race is ajitter with a nervous and mental breakdown. And even the saints have caught the fever of the age and spend most of their time in a glorified much-ado-about-nothing. But we are not here to catch the spirit of the age. We are to counteract the spirit of the age; and many an Elijah, collapsed under the juniper, must be summoned to Horeb to learn the lesson of the still, small voice.

There is a lot of fanfare and activity today and wheels within wheels, but how mediocre we are! There is a flood of words and a famine of ideas. Wheelbarrow preaching is done up in "Rolls Royce" phraseology. For every thought there are five hundred words—where there are any thoughts at all. And no wonder. The preacher's study has become an office. He may want to give himself to the ministry of the Word and prayer, but the times and the trustees have made him an ecclesiastical bellboy and clerical button-pusher. If he shows any signs of leaving the merry-go-round, he is told that times have changed and he must adjust himself. Adjust himself to what? To this Punch-and-Judy farce of modern church life, this St. Vitus dance of the saints, this meaningless marathon of breathless Christians, too exhausted to run and too scared to rest?

The most important and difficult task before the man of God today is to take his life in his teeth and buck popular opinion in order to make more room in his life for God. It is one of the ironies of the ministry that the very man who works in God's name is often hardest put to find time for God. The parents of Jesus lost Him at church, and they were not the last ones to lose Him there. Contrary to popular notion, there is no work more likely to crowd out the quiet hour than the very work that draws its strength from the quiet hour. The clerk in a candy shop often loses his taste for candy; and the person who dispenses the things of God may lose his own love for them in the process. Familiarity may not breed contempt in such a case, but often it breeds neglect. Tending the vineyards of others, we forget our own.

Since the quiet hour spent with God is the preacher's power-house, the devil centers his attack on that source of strength. Laziness, social pleasures, recreations, even a love of good eating, as McCheyne pointed out, can steal the devotional life. And if that fails, the good is allowed to crowd out the best so that in the treadmill of many good things he loses the one thing needful. Unwittingly, the church conspires to rob the preacher of his power, demanding of him such a multitude of small performances that on Sunday he cannot preach at all. To relieve that dilemma, the booksellers supply him with a manual for the year with sermons for both morning and night. Grasping at that, he who began as a preacher ends as a phonograph, reciting mail-order sermons that never breathed the breath of life.

I grant you that in this mechanized, high-pressure, efficiency-expert, quantity-production age, it is a herculean task to make time for the still, small voice. The world, the flesh, and the devil have united against it; and sometimes so have the church members and the deacon board. A man's foes in this regard are sometimes found even among his own household. But it were better to miss a week of committee meetings and pass up a score of "important" appointments and return from Horeb on Sunday morning with a word from the Lord. "Let the dead bury their dead," thundered our Lord long ago, "but go thou and preach the kingdom of God" (Luke 9:60). The preacher who attends too many of this world's funerals is soon the corpse at his own.

The king asked Jeremiah, "Is there any word from the Lord?"

And Jeremiah said, "There is." He paid the price in order to have something to say.

Too often the congregation pitifully looks into the minister's face on Sunday morning and asks the same question. But, to be honest, the dear man would have to reply, "I do not know. I have not had time to find out."

God is on the lookout for the man who will listen.

But he must not only be quiet enough to get a message from God, he must be brave enough to give it.

An old conductor stood at a gate in a railroad station on a bitterly cold night, leisurely punching tickets while restless passengers stamped their feet and grumbled.

"You are an unpopular man tonight, conductor," said one as he passed the gate.

The old conductor replied, "There is only one man with whom I am interested in being in good standing, and that is the superintendent of this railroad."

The man of God needs something of that spirit today.

God pity the preacher who has grown cross-eyed watching certain faces in his congregation to observe whether the message is acceptable or not. "The fear of man bringeth a snare" (Proverbs 29:25), and the chilly countenances of resentful listeners who must not be disturbed have taken the heart out of more preachers than have all the infidels and higher critics. Well did Spurgeon say, "We admire a man who was firm in the faith four hundred years ago, but such a man is a nuisance today."

Stephen might cry in his day, "Ye stiffnecked and uncircumcised in heart and ears, ye do always resist the Holy Ghost" (Acts 7:51), but since that day a lot of books have been written on pulpit behavior and ministerial ethics. The devil has arguments aplenty for toning down the message of the

Lord. Many a preacher starts out to be tactful and ends by being tasteless. He aims at being "balanced," but achieves instead an innocuous collection of harmless sentences that cancel each other's meaning. The congregation goes home having reaped nothing more from the service than a complacent satisfaction with having attended church.

Holy boldness, however, calls attention to the Lord and not to the preacher. They took knowledge of Peter and John, not that they were bold, but that they had been with Jesus. Boldness is prayed down, not worked up. The early church prayed for boldness and got it (Acts 4:29-31). It is not mere recklessness nor ordinary courage. The torch of the Spirit must be upon it. But it is a testimony in itself, for it was the boldness of Peter and John that impressed the listeners. The manner of the messenger is almost as important as the message. A lion of a sermon shrivels when spoken with the spirit of a mouse. Many a man congratulates himself on being meek when he is only scared. Moses was a meek man, but no one ever accused him of timidity once he got down to business.

Now bashfulness and self-consciousness are common, and the saints of old suffered from them. Gideon and Jeremiah and Timothy wrestled with them and by divine help were victorious. Paul had to stir up Timothy on the subject, and many who have followed in his train have known the misery of knocking knees and failing breath before the multitude. It is better to face men so and have God come to the rescue than march into the pulpit haughty and come out humiliated. But the man who has been quiet enough to get a message from God will find in the same quiet hour the grace to give it.

Beware of one other snare. Many a preacher has noticed that just before the time to preach, Satan assails him often with a storm of accusations: "Who are you to be telling other people how to do? You are not so good yourself." If there is no unconfessed and unforsaken sin in the life, disregard such assaults and preach. If you are honest with God and as surrendered as you know how to be, remember that if you waited until you were perfect you would never preach and that you are preaching not yourself but Christ Jesus the Lord.

And this brings us to the third consideration. We must not only be quiet enough to get a message from God and brave enough to give it, we must be honest enough to live it. I say "honest," for it is plain dishonesty to press upon others advice that you have never taken, and rankest hypocrisy to wax eloquent on glorious themes that have never been proved in personal experience.

"Cursed be he that doeth the work of the Lord deceitfully" (Jeremiah 48:10). And if to hear the Word and not do it is to deceive oneself (James 1:22), then twice deceived is he who not only hears but dares to preach what he himself has never practiced. No sermon is so powerful as the preacher's life, and without it the testimony of lip is but sounding brass and clanging cymbal.

We are not merely to teach men what Christ commanded, we are to teach them to observe what He commanded. That we cannot do until we have observed it ourselves. Our Lord told the Pharisees, "Go ye and learn what that meaneth, I will have mercy, and not sacrifice" (Matthew 9:13). They knew where that verse was, but they did not know truly what it was. It was a proverb in their heads but not a practice of their hearts.

Horatius Bonar wrote,

> Thou must be true thyself
> If thou the truth wouldst teach;
> Thy soul must overflow if thou
> Another's soul wouldst reach!
> It takes the overflow of heart
> To give the lips full speech.

Primarily, a sermon is not a work of art but of heart. There are preachers who are "getting up" sermons who need to get them down—down from above. But they must be not only brought down, but also lived out.

An old minister explained the blurs on his sermon outlines by saying they were caused by sweat and tears. And without those two marks, a sermon is not a sermon. Sweat stands for work, and messages from God are not born in naps under a shade tree. Tears stand for compassion born of experience, the sympathy that can comfort others with the comfort wherewith one is comforted of God. It is not enough to love to preach. We must love those to whom we preach, and such love is a practical thing.

God is on the lookout for a man whose heart is perfect toword Him. Will you be quiet enough to hear Him, brave enough to proclaim Him, and honest enough to obey Him?

# THE KIND OF PREACHING WE NEED

A preacher may be wrapped in the robes of learning, and his study walls may be decked with diplomas. His home may be filled with travel souvenirs from many lands, and he may wear all the trappings of ecclesiastical prestige and pageantry. But he cannot function without unction.

# The Kind of Preaching We Need

In these wild and weird and wicked times, the work of the preacher is being rethought and revamped and reexamined. Some think the preacher is just to be an equipper of the laymen for their ministry. He's been pushed from the center of the platform to the wings in favor of celebrated experts and entertainers. But the Book still says, "How shall they hear without a preacher?" (Romans 10:14).

What kind of preaching do we need today? We need the same kind we've always needed. Nothing important has changed. Just because we've split the atom and sent a man to the moon doesn't mean we need a new kind of Christianity. We have a new kind of preacher in some quarters, but we don't need him.

The preaching that we do need is *apostolic*. Of course, there are no apostles today in the original sense, but an apostle is one sent, and a preacher is also a man sent from God. The apostles studied at the feet of Jesus Christ. Our Lord said, "Learn of me," and that means studying in the school of Christ Himself. It's possible to have a magna cum laude from a college and be a first-grader in the school of Jesus Christ.

The apostles were witnesses of and to the resurrection. Paul did not look much like a success in his last days, although he did have stocks and bonds. But the stocks were on his feet and the bonds on his wrists. His only ambition was to know *Him* and the power of *His* resurrection, the fellowship of *His* suffering, and conformity to *His* death. When a preacher or anybody else has moved from "me" and "mine" to "Him" and "His," he is in the apostolic succession.

The apostolic preacher was *anointed* by the Holy Spirit—

divinely appointed and divinely anointed. We have a new Madison Avenue school of the prophets complete with degrees, personality, travel experience, sophisticated methods, up-to-date communication, and public relations; but how many are God-appointed and God-anointed?

In Exodus 30:32-33, instructions are given about the anointing oil for the priests: "Upon man's flesh shall it not be poured. . . . Whosoever compoundeth any like it, or whosoever putteth any of it upon a stranger, shall even be cut off from his people."

One of our problems today is that we're running an old-Adam improvement society. An unsanctified flesh that has never died to sin and risen to walk in newness of life is running down church aisles to rededicate, and God wouldn't use it if you rededicated it a thousand times.

Not many wise, mighty, or noble have been called. Why? "That no flesh should glory in His presence." I wonder how long it's going to take us to learn that they that are in the flesh cannot please God. We've never learned this, but perhaps there has never been as much flesh glorying in His presence as today.

The unction, the anointing oil, is not sold over any counter. Simon Magus tried to buy it, but it was not for sale. It's not compounded by any apothecary; it's not put together by chemistry. A preacher may be wrapped in the robes of learning, and his study walls may be decked with diplomas. His home may be filled with travel souvenirs from many lands, and he may wear all the trappings of ecclesiastical prestige and pageantry. But he cannot function without unction.

John Wesley demonstrated that a long time ago. He began his ministry equipped with formidable qualifications. No man was ever better prepared and less ready to preach. Many a pre-Aldersgate Wesley today starts out to convert the Indian without ever having been converted himself.

Now, when I speak of being anointed by the Holy Spirit, I'm not advocating weird hallucinations, pretending to be the work of the Holy Spirit. When the Holy Spirit becomes the figurehead in any blueprint, that movement becomes eccentric because the business of the Holy Spirit is to magnify Jesus Christ.

But there must be divine enduement; and when God calls a man to apostolic preaching, he must be in the appointed place for his anointing as Matthew 28:16 ("Then the eleven disciples went away into Galilee, into a mountain where Jesus had appointed them") tells us. The appointing and the anointing are God's business. All He asks of the candidate is consent and cooperation. Now that doesn't mean that every one appointed and anointed will be a well-known preacher. He may be pastor of a little country church out at Frog Pond somewhere, but he's qualified to the task God gave him to do.

The preaching that we need today must be *authoritative*. My Lord taught us having authority and not as the scribes. Too much today sounds like the scribes. There's no king in Israel; every man does what is right in his own eyes. Authority goes out, and anarchy comes in. Jesus met the devil not in His own name, not in His own power, but with the Scriptures: "It is written. . . . It is written. . . . It is written." If He could defeat the devil with three verses out of Deuteronomy, we ought to be able to do it with the whole Bible.

Don't be ashamed of the old-time religion. There is nothing newer. We have a New Testament about a new and living way. We enter that way by new birth. We are new creatures with a new name and a new song, walking in newness of life, living by a new commandment, headed for a new heaven and a new earth and a new Jerusalem. And almost the last word of the New Testament in Revelation 21:5 is, "Behold, I make all things new." No wonder the gospel is good news old time, new time, any time, all the time. God is not running an antique shop. "These things speak, and exhort, and rebuke with all authority. Let no man despise thee" (Titus 2:15) .

But you can't preach it like it is if you don't believe it like it was. If you don't believe that the Scriptures are God-breathed and that Jesus Christ was virgin born, that He died for our sins and rose bodily from the grave and is coming again, you can't preach it like it is. You can't preach "Jesus Christ the same yesterday" today, if you don't believe what He was yesterday. For what He was then He is now.

We must not be apologetic, with an inferiority complex in the presence of the new left and the hippies and the jet set. I heard a great black preacher say before twenty-five hundred preachers, "I don't belong to the right wing or the left wing. They're both flapping on the same old bird."

I tell you that if anybody's embarrassed today, it oughtn't be the preachers. It ought to be that other crowd. We don't have to call in TV celebrities and athletic personalities to put the gospel over. We're trying to fix up something that doesn't need fixing up. We're trying to gild the lily and paint the sunset, hobnob with Sodom, and get chummy with Gomorrah. You don't have to go to the love-ins to find out what the hippies are thinking, or drink gingerale at the country clubs to find out what that crowd's thinking.

What difference does it make what they're thinking? God says, "My thoughts are not your thoughts, neither are your ways my ways" (Isaiah 55:8). The only thing that matters is what God is thinking and what God is saying. Some of these avant-garde boys ought to wake up.

The devil told me a long time ago that if I didn't get with it I'd have nowhere to preach, that I'd starve to death. Now from the way I look, you may think the devil's right; but I'm getting on all right. I'm busier at seventy than I ever was at fifty, and some of these dear fellows who are knocking themselves out trying to keep up with the procession ought to get up to date. We don't need anything new so much as we need something so old it'd be new if anybody tried it.

They tell us we need a new lingo today. We must learn the new terminology. Instead of a problem, it's a "hang-up." Instead of a blessing, it's a "meaningful experience." We must be relevant, communicate, dialogue with the now, study the spectrum, seek fulfillment in involvement, and get down to the nitty-gritty.

What difference does it make what they call it? They used to call it "itch" and now it's "allergy," but you scratch just the same. Too many people are stamping their feet and clapping their hands and singing "hallelujah" without the slightest idea what they're singing "hallelujah" about. They're getting on every bandwagon that goes by without asking who's at the head of the parade and where it's going.

Instead of setting the pattern, the professing church is tagging along today, imitating every new fad that comes by. If those things were so good, why didn't we lead? Why weren't we up in the cab instead of back in the caboose? You don't have to put on mod attire and pick a guitar and stage rock operas and drop all the way from hymns to hootenannies.

They tell us now that Isaac Watts did not speak the idiom of today. Well, neither did Shakespeare, but they're still studying him. It's an insult to the intelligence of young people to give them the impression you have to cheapen the gospel to make it understandable. The medical schools do not simplify their phraseology to please this set. The legal profession hasn't changed its terminology. The young people of this generation are perfectly capable of comprehending—as the Holy Spirit reveals it—the truth of God.

All the church needs to do is be the church. God never told a church to be an accompanist. He called the church to be a soloist. We have our own song to sing; we don't have to sing anybody else's song. They say the end justifies the means. But the means determines the end. And if the means are unworthy, they spoil the end before you even get started.

When Spurgeon was preaching, Barnum and Bailey offered him a fat price to come over here and preach. And I know what we'd say today. We'd say, "Why don't you go? The devil's had the money long enough. Why don't you go over and preach?"

But not Mr. Spurgeon. He answered with Acts 13:10, "O full of all subtilty and all mischief, thou child of the devil, thou enemy of all righteousness, wilt thou not cease to pervert the right ways of the Lord?" But then, we don't have many Spurgeons. We plunge frantically in all directions trying to popularize the gospel.

The Ichabod Memorial Church decides to pack them in with folk music. And then they say over at Ephesus, "Well, we'll try a TV personality." Then Pergamos says, "Well, we're gonna have a fella who can play a fiddle and beat tap drums and blow a harmonica all at the same time." Then over at Sardis they say, "We're gonna put on Aunt Dinah's quilting party. Come dressed like they were a hundred years ago, and we'll all see Nellie home." Then over at Laodicea they have a talking horse.

I heard of one of those horses some time ago. They asked him how many commandments, and he stomped ten times. How many apostles, and he stomped twelve times. Some nitwit in the crowd asked how many hypocrites there are in this church, and he went into a dance on all fours.

We're living in a fog, and we can't distinguish the divine from the demonic. All we need to do is assert our delegated authority as preachers and preach the Word in the power of the Spirit. It must be authoritative. "If any man speak, let him speak as the oracles of God" (1 Peter 4:11).

Then it must be *absolute*. This is a day of relativism. Right used to be right, and wrong used to be wrong. Now black and white have been smudged into indefinite gray. We've had two wars that we've neither won nor lost. We're afraid to win them and ashamed to lose them. But General Douglas MacArthur summed it up when he said, "There's no substitute for victory."

Joseph Parker said of Spurgeon, "The only colors Mr. Spurgeon knew were black and white. In all things he was definite. You were either in or out, up or down, alive or dead."

Beloved, we're dealing in absolutes. The absolute authority

of the Scriptures, the absolute lordship of Jesus Christ, the absolute sovereignty of the Holy Spirit. It sounds too dogmatic to some people today because they blow from dogma to smogma. They're living in a fog.

Jesus Christ was and is absolute. He said, "He that is not with me is against me; and he that gathereth not with me scattereth abroad" (Matthew 12:30). You'll observe there's no third class there, and there's no such thing as an inactive church member. If you're not gathering, if you're not drawing people to Christ, you are driving them away from Christ; you are scattering. Sin is dogmatic. Death is dogmatic. Hell is dogmatic.

I remember when the *Titanic* sank in 1912, it was the ship that was supposed to be unsinkable. The only thing it ever did was sink. When it took off from England, all kinds of passengers were aboard—millionaires, celebrities, people of moderate means, and poor folks down in the steerage. But a few hours later when they put the list in the Cunard office in New York, it carried only two categories—lost and saved. Tragedy had crossed out all other distinctions.

Out on life's sea there are scores of classifications. But when the voyage is over, it won't matter whether you were a rich man, poor man, beggar man, thief, butcher, baker, candlestick maker, whether you lived in the backwoods or on the boulevard, whether you drove a Cadillac or pushed an apple cart to town. All such distinctions disappear and only two lists remain—lost and saved. We're dealing with absolutes.

But whereas our preaching is authoritative and absolute, it ought to be *affectionate*. "Speaking the truth in love" (Ephesians 4:15). Some preach the truth and don't have love. Some preach love and don't have the truth. Get the mixture right. You have to mix it. A man puts one foot in hot water and the other foot in ice water and feel very uncomfortable. But when he mixes the waters, he's quite all right.

The truth will keep you from dissolving into sentimentality; love will keep you from hardening into severity. Truth will keep you from turning to sugar, and love will keep you from turning to vinegar. The Lord preserves His saints; He doesn't pickle them. The Lord drove the money-changers from the Temple and wept over Jerusalem with a broken heart. I don't want to finish my course hard and embittered. I've seen some examples. It's a snare of the devil and a very poor advertisement for the gospel.

Finally, it ought to be *apocalyptic* preaching. It ought to sound like the book of Revelation, for we are living in a grand and awful time, in an age when to be living is sublime.

I heard a preacher take Luke 21:28 as his text, "When these things begin to come to pass, then look up, and lift up your heads; for your redemption draweth nigh." But he went on to say, "In this new time of brotherhood and socialism through educational legislation under religious auspices in the social gospeler's paradise, just as the crocuses are coming up so we are beholding the dawn of a new era."

I couldn't help saying, "Lord, have mercy on any preacher who can live in a cataclysmic hour like this and then stand in the pulpit croaking about crocuses." I'm glad I got my eschatology straightened out a long time ago. I didn't believe it quite like I do now, but God cured me, and I've been immunized against a relapse. May that be the experience of every preacher today.

Beloved, we're living in a terrible time, in a day of beasts and seals and trumpets and four horsemen and the harlot on the beast and scorpions and dragons and a sea of glass mingled with fire and earthquakes and falling stars and Babylon and the bottomless pit and the lake of fire and Gog and Magog and six-six-six and the downfall of the devil and the great white city coming down.

It's no time to tiptoe through the tulips in the ministrative end. In such an hour, good news is bad news and bad news is good news. "When they shall say peace and safety" sounds like good news, but no: "Destruction cometh."

Good news is bad news. "But when you see all these things

come to pass, famines, wars and rumors of wars, men's hearts failing them for fear," that is bad news. But "lift up your heads; for your redemption draweth nigh."

It's exactly the other way around for the Christian. I'm not waiting for the abolition of war and poverty or urban renewal. I'm living in the great "until." If somebody asks you what time it is, tell him it's "until." He might look at you funny, but it will give you a chance to get in a word. We are living in the great "until":

"He which hath begun a good work in you will perform it *until* the day of Jesus Christ" (Philippians 1:6).

I'm waiting *"until* he [that hindereth] be taken out of the way" (2 Thessalonians 2:7).

I'm judging "nothing before the time, *until* the Lord come" (1 Corinthians 4:5).

I'm waiting *"until* the times of the Gentiles be fulfilled" (Luke 21:24).

I'm waiting *"till* he Hath put all enemies under His feet" (1 Corinthians 15:25).

I'm waiting *until* He subdues "all things unto Himself" (Philippians 3:21).

I want to "be sincere and without offense *till* the day of Jesus Christ" (Philippians 1:10).

I want to "hold fast" what I have *until* He comes (Revelation 2:25).

And when I partake of the Lord's Supper, I "show the Lord's death *till* He come" (1 Corinthians 11:26).

And He told me, "Occupy *till* I come" (Luke 19:13).

I'm waiting "until" His enemies be made His footstool (Psalm 110:1).

I preached down in Georgia along that line some time ago. A fine layman wrote a letter to me, and instead of signing it, "Yours truly," or, "Sincerely," he just signed it, "Until." That's a good way to sign a letter.

How is He going to subdue all things and make all His enemies His footstool? By the preaching of the gospel? No.

By social action? No. By building better hogpens out in the far country instead of getting the prodigal home? No.

Somebody said the other day, "When you're up to your ears in crocodiles, it's no time to discuss draining the swamp."

How's He going to subdue all things? When He comes—cataclysmically, apocalyptically, and suddenly.

He's not coming to hold a summit conference with His enemies. He's not coming to reconcile. He did that the first time. He's coming to destroy and conquer and subdue. The day of reconciliation will be over; the day of retribution will begin.

The first time He came quietly, a babe in Bethlehem. He did not cry aloud, and His voice was not heard in the streets.

The next time there will be a shout, the voice of an archangel, and the trump of God to wake the dead. People used to ask how an angel's voice and a trumpet sound could be heard around the world. You don't ask that now. A man can blow a trumpet in New York and be heard in Australia. Our eardrums have been shattered by the devilish dissonance of rock and roll and even gospel jazz. And if a man can blow a trumpet loud enough to deafen the living, God's angel ought to be able to blow one loud enough to waken the dead.

I'm not looking for signs. We've had plenty of them. I'm listening for a sound. Every time you see a scoffer who says there are no signs of His coming, you've just seen another sign. I'm listening for a shout.

It's a great day for preaching—apostolic, authoritative, absolute, affectionate, and apocalyptic.

"Even so, come, Lord Jesus."

## THAT OTHER GOSPEL

If they had had a social gospel in the days of the prodigal son, somebody would have given him a bed and a sandwich and he never would have gone home.

# That Other Gospel

We live in a day of sorcery and demonic deception. The world is tricked and fascinated under the spell of a thousand evil eyes. The weird and the uncanny and the occult flourish. Psychedelic and hallucinatory drugs abound, and humanity is being swept into an orgy of endless insanity.

We've always had fortune tellers and necromancers and magicians. But they are small fry today, for we are being bewitched on a gigantic scale by demonic hosts from the world of darkness. False Christs and false prophets would deceive, if it were possible, the very elect.

In another day the Galatian Christians were bewitched into compromising the gospel with legalism and Judaism. Writing them, Paul declared that he was astonished that they had so soon turned to another gospel, which he said was not another (Galatians 1:6-7). He was so concerned that he wrote in verse 8 and repeated it in verse 9, "If we or an angel preach any other gospel . . . let him be accursed."

Now this early legalistic heterodox is not the only false gospel that has arisen to plague the church. We are beset today by other gospels (which are not other), and Paul might well marvel again at how quickly twentieth-century Christians have been led astray.

There is a new liberal gospel. Liberalism and modernism are not new, but they have changed with the times. We have a brand that may speak the language of orthodoxy, but doesn't mean the same. Harry Emerson Fosdick was honest enough to say that he did not believe in the virgin birth, but today new gospelers conceal their beliefs and sound the chimes like fundamentalists while their leaven permeates our great church today.

These new liberals do not believe as we do, but instead of leaving us and joining groups they do agree with, they infect and infest the great denominations with the malignancy of unbelief. Unfortunately, we have among true believers some who are so tolerant and broadminded as to believe we ought to include in our fellowship all grades and shades of doctrine. They would turn the Lord's sheepfold into a zoo.

When we have room enough for any and every brand of doctrine, that's too much room. Can the same fountain send forth both bitter water and sweet? Can two walk together except they be agreed? One scholar says that the early Christians condemned false doctrine in a way that sounds almost unchristian today. I don't believe that the gospel ship ought to be surrendered to the mutineers. We were here first, and if anybody leaves, let it be the dissenters.

The New Testament has a lot to say about false teachers. It advocates measures that sound stern and harsh to complacent, permissive apostles of compromise from whose pulpits sound travels a lot faster than light. These false gospelers are bewitched by error, and those who tolerate them are bewitched by false tolerance they mistake for Christian charity.

Today there is also the worldly, or secular, gospel, a popular mixture of Christianity and worldliness, a notion that we can be Christians and worldlings both. Our churches are filled with those folk. We call them worldly Christians, or we used to. We would run with the hare and hunt with the hounds, speak out of both sides of the mouth and work both sides of the street. Separation from the world is becoming a discarded doctrine, and there is now a new gospel of earthly prosperity under Christian auspices, as though God wants every man to be rich.

The New Testament image of the Christian is that of a pilgrim and a stranger, an exile and an alien. His citizenship is in heaven. He is not a citizen of earth on his way to heaven; he is a citizen of heaven trying to get through this world. But he has been replaced by a new hail-fellow-well-met, sipping gingerale at cocktail parties, rich and increased with goods and needing nothing in a country-club Christianity.

Such people are bewitched and charmed by the world's delight. Things that are higher and nobler have never allured their sight. Never has the spell of this age fascinated so many Christians as in these days of affluence, when men would serve both God and mammon. Not only does this worldly gospel show up in our lives, it has got into the work of the church. The social world and the business world and the entertainment world have been invited to participate and Hollywood has been called in to help us out. Movie stars play the parts of Bible characters. I'd just as soon listen to a gangster lecture on armistice.

Television actors appear in evangelistic meetings one week and filthy shows the next. Dance programs feature hymns. Gospel rock and Christian combos and hippie evangelists abound. Jazz bands play in staid old sanctuaries, and the church that used to go to the jungle is now seeing the jungle brought into the church. America is amusement and entertainment mad, and we have the highest per capita rate of boredom of any people on the face of the earth. There's a delusion going around today, even in evangelical and fundamental circles sometimes, that we must be entertained at church. Christianity has come all the way from an experience to a performance.

This fusion of the church and the world is the masterpiece of demonic deception in these last days as we are being readied for Babylon and Antichrist. One might ask again, "Who hath bewitched you?" At a rate never known before, Demas is forsaking Paul, having loved this present world.

Then we have in the third place the so-called social gospel. We have had it for years, but there's a new upsurge polarizing our churches today. The new social gospelers say that this is just evangelical Christianity catching up on its obligations to society, that we've been giving priority to the vertical man-to-God relationship and not willing to get up-to-date on the horizontal man-to-man relationship.

Well, this is the course the social gospel has always followed, and I predict that as this epidemic spreads, there will be less and less man-to-God emphasis and more and more man-to-man emphasis. Christianity has always had social implications. The greatest advances in social betterment have followed great spiritual awakenings like the Wesleyan revival. That's one thing; but it's something else when the church becomes a party to political movements masquerading as moral issues.

Some well-meaning but misguided people are easily duped into riding in a bandwagon headed for the promised land, and they'll endorse any effort to produce a counterfeit Millennium and superimpose a false kingdom of heaven on an unregenerate society. The main problem as always is the man-to-God relationship, and when you are right vertically, you will be right horizontally. When you love God, you will love your neighbor.

Today, they tell us our main trouble is environment, and therefore we must major on changing that environment. So we're going out for bigger and better hogpens in a far country instead of getting the prodigal home to the father's house. If they had had a social gospel in the days of the prodigal son, somebody would have given him a bed and a sandwich and he never would have gone home.

Civilization is not going to be Christianized. It ought to be evangelized. There's a right involvement, and there's a wrong involvement. There's a right way to identify with society and a wrong way. Our Lord told us what this is in John 17:18 and once and for all located us in this world. We've been saved out of it to go right back into it to win other people out of it, and that's the only business we have in it.

Meanwhile, we have a great lack of spiritual discernment. One of the most neglected verses today is 1 John 4:1, "Beloved, believe not every spirit, but try the spirits whether they are of God: because many false prophets are gone out into the world."

We're living in a fog in the strangest, weirdest, most uncanny period in the history of the church. Black and white have become gray. Church leaders are lost in the midst, and, unless God raises up some prophets and seers who can see through this smog, then evangelical Christianity faces deterioration and disintegration. You can put the facts together, but the problem is more than the sum of all its parts. The witchery of these times is so charming and pleasant and magical and such good men endorse it that it seems downright unchristian to question it.

I know there is such a thing as attributing the work of God to the devil, as the Pharisees did when they said our Lord worked by the power of Beelzebub. That's a hideous and an awful thing; but is it not possible, as we approach Antichrist, to turn that coin around and attribute the work of the devil to God? Antichrist himself will claim to be God. That's the drift of the age, and agonizing decisions will have to be made.

For Christians who know their Bibles, this shouldn't be any surprise. We've been warned long in advance. "Let us not sleep, as do others; but let us watch and be sober. For they that sleep sleep in the night; and they that be drunken are drunken in the night" (1 Thessalonians 5:6-7).

Get on your breastplate and put on your helmet, and stand up, stand up for Jesus. The strife will not be long.

I heard some time ago of some small boys who were marching in a parade, and one little fellow was out of step with all the rest. Closer investigation revealed that he had a transistor radio under his coat, and he was marching to music a thousand miles away. That's the way the Christian ought to go through this old world—out of step with its music and its movement, marching to the drumbeat of another realm.

Don't be afraid to be out of step. This world has to square with the gospel. Gilbert K. Chesterson said, "The world has been moved most by men who contradicted it most." My Lord is not standing around with His hat in His hand, waiting for our approval. We must all appear before His judgment seat.

# A HOLY MAN OF GOD PASSED BY

There's a price to pay to be a holy man of God.
You have to buck the current because the tide's
running the other way.

# A Holy Man of God Passed By

One of the finest tributes ever paid a man occurs in 2 Kings 4:9. You remember that Elisha had visited in the home of a Shunammite, and the lady of the house suggested to her husband that they fix up a prophet's chamber for him, for "I perceive that this is an holy man of God, which passeth by us continually."

My first pastorate was a country church back in the twenties. I was a bachelor then, and I was a pedestrian. I didn't own a car. I didn't buy an automobile until I was sixty-six. I wanted to think it over. I did a lot of walking in those days. This is the day of the motorist, and any man who walks is viewed with suspicion. You see a man coming down the road now just meditating, and you figure he's either out of his head or out of gas, one of the two. He's such a rarity that dogs bark as though they'd seen a ghost, and policemen have been known to follow a pedestrian for blocks to make sure he isn't up to something.

One memory lingers from that pastorate. Along my route there was a grocery store, and the grocer said one day, "Preacher, I want you to know that many a time when things were not going well, I looked out my store widow and saw you going by, and it helped. I felt better." He didn't elaborate on that, but I've never forgotten it. It's been my prayer that souls along my way, as I went through the years, might be able to say to some small degree what this Shunammite woman said, "I perceive that this is a holy man of God that passeth by us continually."

That ought to be the ambition of every Christian on his pilgrimage through this world. Luke tells us that when our Lord was on His way to Jericho, somebody told a blind man,

"Jesus of Nazareth passeth by." He's still passing by, but not as then. He passes by in His people and particularly in His preachers. He has no hands, no feet but ours; and if this world reads the gospel, it'll be the gospel according to you and me— for most of them don't read Matthew, Mark, Luke, and John.

In this same pastorate, I heard a great deal about an old minister of years before by the name of Josiah Hilliard. There had been ministers in that church who went on to prominent pulpits, and I didn't hear much about them. I kept hearing about Josiah Hilliard. I knew he was a very poor man who had given what little he had to help boys through school, but I wondered what was the secret of his strength.

I decided I'd ask my farmer friend, John Brown. He was an unusual character, never in a hurry, who always had time to think. He plowed back there on the creek, and I made my way through that cypress swamp one afternoon. Oh, I spent many an afternoon talking to John Brown. He should have been plowing, and I should have been visiting, but we'd talk all afternoon, and then I'd come back next morning. We never said, "Good morning." We just took up where we'd left off the day before and went on with our conversation.

I said to him, "John, all I hear about is Josiah Hilliard. Now you've had preachers that I have heard about, but these people talk about Josiah Hilliard. What was the secret of his strength and the grip he had on you folks?"

John leaned on the plow handle and thought a moment. "He just loved us." Then he went on plowing and left me standing there.

I made my way back through that cypress swamp while the woodthrush was singing his vespers at the end of a perfect day, and there chimed in my heart something that said, "Though I speak with the tongues of men and of angels, and have not love, it profiteth me nothing."

And I said, "Lord, help me to move into the middle of the thirteenth chapter of First Corinthians and settle down for the duration." That's a good place to live.

Josiah Hilliard was a holy man of God who passed by continually.

In this psychedelic age, the term *man of God* indicates wild and weird and woolly freaks. But in the Bible it meant a man who kept company with the Almighty. Elijah could say to Ahab, "As the Lord God of Israel liveth before whom I stand . . ." When you're accustomed to standing before God, kings don't matter much. Big potentates are just small potatoes when you have been standing in the presence of the Most High.

The Shunammite woman didn't say, "I perceive that this is a famous man of God, or a popular, or brilliant, or successful man of God." She said a "holy" man of God.

Now, since the words "holy" and "holiness" have fallen on evil days, they've become a byword. They've come to mean fanaticism and emotional excesses, rolling in the hay and foaming at the mouth. Some who have preached the highest standards have sunk the lowest in practice, and we've shied away in horror. We've fallen into a snare of the devil by so doing. Every Bible doctrine has been carried to extremes at one time or another. Just because some folks go into wildfire doesn't mean the rest of us have to live in a deep freeze. We don't have to freeze, and we don't have to fry. One thing is certain. The Bible is so full of those words "holy" and "holiness" that it takes several pages of a concordance to list them. I undertook to check them sometime ago and gave up. From the high priest who wore "Holiness unto the Lord" on his forehead to the multitude in Revelation crying, "Holy, holy, holy, Lord God Almighty," this Book deserves to be called a Holy Bible. Whether you like holiness or not, you'd better, because without holiness no man shall see the Lord.

There's a new variety of preacher today who's not interested in being called "a holy man of God." He wants to be called by his first name and be just one of the boys. He's so anxious to be relevant that he's forgotten how to be reverent. I never cared for "Reverend" as a title, but it does indicate some respect. If this Shunammite woman had heard Elisha tell the jokes some preachers tell at civic club luncheons, she would never have given us this text.

Some time ago, somebody said, "But you don't have to wear a halo to be a Christian." No, and you don't have to wear a great big button saying, "I'm a Christian," or carry a Bible the size of a Chicago telephone directory. But the Bible says Christians belong to a holy nation. We ought to show by countenance and conversation and conduct some of the characteristics of our heavenly nationality.

Too often, we smile at low business standards, laugh at fashionable jests, tolerate ambiguous pleasures, and soften everything to a comfortable acquiescence. We seek to be all things to all men to please all. We run with the hare while we hunt with the hounds. We're victims of illicit compromise. There's nothing distinctive about our character. We wear gray when we mix with the businessmen of the congregation and talk gray in conversation with them. It's a sad day for a preacher when he's mortally afraid somebody will think he is a preacher. And it's a sad day for any Christian when he's afraid somebody will think he is a Christian.

We're living in a day when tragedy has become comedy. We're laughing at things that ought to make us cry. The cause of Jesus Christ has been hurt more by unwise jokesters than by all the infidels. I marvel at the jesting and flippant remarks I hear sometimes during revival.

You remember that, in 2 Samuel 6, when Uzzah tried to steady the Ark, he dropped dead. Have you ever studied out what exactly was his sin? It must have been pretty serious for God to strike a man dead.

Well, for one thing, he was the son of Abinadab, and all his life the Ark had been in his house. It was a familiar piece of furniture. He'd seen it all those years, and the Ark had become to him just a box. He'd lost regard for the sacredness of it as a symbol of God's presence among His people. Old Matthew Henry says, "Perhaps he effected to show before this great assembly how bold he could [be] with the Ark having been so long acquainted with it." Familiarity even with that which is most awful is apt to breed contempt.

Uzzah was a Levite, but he wasn't a priest. Only the priest could touch the Ark (Numbers 4:15), and that only under certain circumstances.

We're not Levites; we're priests. The Scriptures teach the priesthood of the believers. But it's a sad day, my friend, when the Ark becomes a box, and you become so familiar with Scripture and worship and the ordinances that you lose your reverence.

Alexander MacLaren said, "It was a low sense of awe in the case of Uzzah." Nothing is more delicate than the sense of awe. Trifle with it ever so little, and it speedily disappears. Watch the average Sunday morning congregation. You don't see much awe there. What you see is not awe; it's awful. Relevance has become more important than reverence. You can take God's name in vain in church because you don't have to cuss to do it. You can do it when you stand and sing, "My Jesus, I love Thee, I know Thou art mine; / For Thee all the follies of sin I resign," if you haven't done it. You do it when you sing, "Have Thine own way, Lord! / Have Thine own way," and you don't mean it.

A tourist in Africa chanced on some boys playing marbles. At closer look he discovered they were playing with diamonds. That was where diamonds were mined. Playing marbles with diamonds! We're doing that in church today.

I read of a girl who, touring Europe, went to Vienna to the museum where Beethoven's piano is displayed. This poor little thing sat down and played some rock and roll on it. The old caretaker endured it, and after it was over, he said, "Paderewski was through here some years ago."

"Oh?" she said, "and what did he play?"

"Nothing," the caretaker said. "He said he was not worthy to touch Beethoven's piano."

I'm sure that poor little thing must have gone out of there red in the face, if she was capable of embarrassment.

It's awful to treat the Ark like a box and to cheapen with familiarity the holy things of God. Watch that. Somebody has said, "There's no greater hindrance to true spirituality than a superficial acquaintance with the language of Christianity from childhood."

Now that sounds like a rather questionable statement, but I've thought it over. I grew up in a Christian home, and I thank God for it; but it's dangerous. I read through the New Testament, I don't know how many times, when I was a very small boy. I have articles I wrote for the paper when I was nine. I was licensed to preach at eleven and ordained when I was fifteen. But there came a day when I had to back myself into a corner and say, "Hey, you, is this real, or is it something you learned until you can recite it? Is this real to you?"

If we ever have a confrontation with a holy God and if God ever visits us again in true revival, it will end this prostitution of holy things. We'll be red with embarrassment about some of the silly things we've been doing to try to put the gospel over.

Oh, you say, we must relate and communicate to the new age. Well, we're not doing it too well with all the new techniques. We're not cutting the mustard. We're preaching happiness instead of holiness. God didn't save you to make you happy. That's a by-product. He saved you to make you holy. You were predestinated to be conformed to the image of God's Son. If you want to be popular, preach happiness. If you want to be unpopular, preach holiness.

Oh, you say, but doesn't the Bible tell us that "if ye know these things, happy are ye if ye do them?" Yes, but it's conditioned on two if's—knowing the Word of God and doing the will of God. There's a price to pay to be a holy man of God. You have to buck the current because the tide's running the other way.

Now what was the secret of Elisha, the holy man of God?

Remember that day when Elijah was to be translated? This prophet who had lived his life in a furious tempest was going to heaven in a fiery whirlwind, and Elisha made up his mind to be there when it happened.

Elijah tried to shake him off at Bethel and at Jericho and at Jordan, but Elisha said, "I will not leave thee." He knew he was the successor to Elijah. He wanted a double portion—not twice as much, but the elder brother's portion. And the person God honors today is the one who won't be put off with anything less than the best God has for him.

Now on the road that day were some seminary students, and they knew something was going to happen. They inquired about it, fifty of them stood to view it afar off, but nothing happened to them. That's as close as some people ever get to a double portion of God's blessing. They hear about it, talk about it; they're in the vicinity. But they never see the chariots of fire. Elijah's mantle is not for them.

Beloved, it is not enough to live in the neighborhood of a miracle. Holy men of God don't live on hearsay, on second-hand experiences. There are plenty of schools of the prophets these days along the roadside, gossiping like these young prophets did. But it's only once in a while that an Elisha says, "I'm going through to a double portion and into the prophet's mantle."

You remember what he said to those preachers, "Hold your peace." Men who are in dead earnest don't engage in idle chatter with roadside reverends. Elijah's translation wasn't a subject for idle speculation; it wasn't a temporary excitement. Elisha knew it was for him the opportunity of a lifetime, and if he blew it he'd be an ordinary preacher the rest of his days.

A Christian who's out for God's best doesn't have any time to waste on bystanders. Some stop at Bethel, and some stop at Jericho, and some never get to Jordan because they talk it over with the schools of the prophets. The Christian who is out for the prophet's mantle will do well to say, "All ye who verily talk about it, hold your peace." Don't you let anybody stop you short of God's best for you. Elisha went the distance that makes the difference.

Do you remember what Ruth said to Naomi? "I'm going through. Entreat me not to leave thee." Orpah kissed her mother-in-law, but Ruth clave unto her. We've got a lot of saints today who give the Lord a kiss once in a while. God wants people who say like Ruth, "Whither thou goest, I will go; and where thou lodgest, I will lodge: thy people shall be my people, and thy God my God" (Ruth 1:16). She went on to be the great-grandmother of David and an ancestress of the Lord Jesus Christ.

Judas betrayed my Lord, not with a slap but with a kiss. And Jesus Christ is being betrayed today more with a kiss than a slap. We notice the slaps and say, "Isn't that awful!" But many people give Him a kiss of respect and never follow Him.

Have you gone the distance that makes the difference?

I was preaching in the mountains of East Tennessee one summer and got up every morning before breakfast to climb one of those mountains. It was a little rough, and I got about halfway when discretion told me that maybe I ought to settle for that since I was no longer young. But I saw a light place up among the trees, and I said, "I believe if I reach it, there'll be a view."

And I made it. I stood there early in the morning and looked out on that unforgettable sight. I said, "Well, the difference is worth the effort." And it is.

And that extra mile of prayer, that extra time with your Bible, that extra season of communion is worth the effort.

> My heart has no desire to stay
>   Where doubts arise and fears dismay;
> Though some may dwell where these abound,
>   My prayer, my aim is higher ground.*

It's that extra mile that gets through to God's best.

Then the Shunammite woman said, "This is a man of God,

*Johnson Oatman, Jr.

a holy man of God, that passeth by us continually." Elisha didn't hide in a cave and polish his halo. He walked among men. Our Lord didn't spend His days lecturing in some secluded spot. He went about doing good. He was always passing by, and so must we. If we say we abide in Him, we ought to walk as He walked. Our walk must match our talk.

Elisha was available to everybody from kings to commoners, and they all beat a path to his door. He solved the water problem at Jericho, put a prophet's wife in the oil business at a profit, raised a Shunammite's son, healed Naaman of his leprosy, purified the poison in a pot, recovered an axehead, relieved a famine, anointed Jehu, and led the Syrians blind into Samaria. After he died and long after he'd been buried, they lowered somebody else's corpse onto the bones of that old prophet, and that fellow came to. Why, Elisha's corpse even woke the dead. I tell you that old preacher had a lot of vitality in his system. He had more power dead than the rest of us have living. He made a trail of blessing.

I love the Ozarks in the springtime. One year, an old mountain missionary took me way back beyond, back in the hills to show me his work and tell me about his predecessor who used to drive an old, ramshackled automobile down those crooked trails. He had an amplifier attached, and he'd come down those crooked roads singing at the top of his voice: "I know the Lord will make a way for me."

They say the mountain folk would stop whatever they were doing and listen. And then they'd say, "That's the missionary going home." That's a great way to go home, brother. That's the way I want to go home. I want somebody to be able to say along the way, " 'Twas a holy man of God that passed by here."

Another character who used to be around Moody Bible Institute I thought so much of. It was Homer Hammontree. He grew up in little old Greenback, Tennessee. He sang the gospel all over the land and taught music here. Out of the hills he came and back to the hills he went. All his life he was just a big old Tennessee mountain boy.

Well, last fall I was preaching in Johnson City and Knoxville and Maryville, and I said to the preacher, "Where is Greenback, Tennessee?"

He said, "Oh, it's not far out here."

I said, "Let's go over there."

I found the country cemetery, and I found Hammontree's grave. He never married. He lay there alone behind a big shade tree, and on that tombstone are words that I believe are on Mr. Moody's tombstone: "The world passeth away, and the lusts thereof: but he that doeth the will of God abideth forever" (1 John 2:17). The last time I heard Hammontree sing, he and Paul Beckwith sang "The Story of Jesus Will Never Grow Old."

It's good to grow old singing a song that will never grow old, an ageless theme that the years cannot dim nor time outdate.

"He that doeth the will of God." That's success. That's fulfillment. If a man has missed that, he's failed, though his corpse be housed in the stateliest mausoleum. If he does God's will, he's a success, though he rest at the finish in a country churchyard out in the hills.

Well, I came from those hills just across the line in North Carolina not far. And when my journey's over, I could wish to go back to those hills. I could wish that all whose lives I've touched along the way might be able to say to some degree, "I perceive that this was a holy man of God who passed by us continually."

## HOME BEFORE DARK

Even in the stiff, formal churches we've swung
all the way from rigor mortis to St. Vitus.

# Home Before Dark

Too many people assemble at God's house who don't really believe in the power of God. Having begun in the Spirit, we live in the flesh.

I heard of a boy's school where every morning before classes the youngsters were supposed to recite the Apostles' Creed. Each one was given a segment of the creed: "I believe in God the Father Almighty," and so on down the line.

One morning they were getting along pretty well until all at once there was a dead stop and a profound silence. Then a lad spoke up and said, "The boy who believes in the Holy Ghost is not here this morning."

I'm afraid that's happened in a lot of church prayer meetings these days.

I heard of a pastor who met one of his delinquent members and said, "Well, I haven't seen you in church much lately."

"No," he said, "you know how it's been. The children have been sick, and then it's rained and rained and rained."

The pastor said, "Well, it's always dry at church."

"Yeah," he said, "that's another reason why I haven't been coming."

It ought not be so. We are dealing with divine dynamite, and I believe that everyone who comes to every service ought to get a blessing and go out charged up.

But when we study the genesis and genius of Christianity, one thing stands out: God's ways are not our ways, and His thoughts are not our thoughts. The way He demonstrated His plan and purpose and the way He set it up both utterly contradict our sophisticated ways of staging great events today.

If we had been on the committee of arrangements, think how

we would have planned the coming of the Son of God. Why, who would ever have suggested His coming as a baby born in a stable in an obscure corner of the Roman Empire? We would have had Him brought to earth full grown to lecture in Rome and Alexandria and Athens. And at twelve in the Temple, what a chance He missed to be known as the famous boy preacher. How our modern publicity agents would have exploited that. With the whole world to save, why did He spend thirty of those precious years in a carpenter shop? He could have visited the known world all those years.

When He did start out, His brothers said in John 7, "Why don't you go up to Jerusalem? Get out of the backwoods and get up on the boulevards where they can hear of you. You're not handling your publicity right."

He said, "The world can't hate you because you belong to it, but me it hateth because I testify of it that its works are evil."

When that demoniac was healed and wanted to join the evangelistic party, Jesus said, "No, you go home and tell them what God has done for you." What a chance they had to take this ex-demoniac along. Think what an attraction he would have been: "Ex-wild man will be at the next meeting!"

When Jesus performed a miracle, He sometimes said, "Don't tell it." He performed miracles but didn't advertise them; we advertise them and don't perform them. When He chose the twelve disciples, why didn't He start at the top instead of with a band of nonentities reeking with the smell of fish and the taint of tax-collecting—no pedigree and not photogenic? We wouldn't have looked at them a second time.

When He arose, why didn't He appear before Pilate and Herod and say, "All right, here I am"? What a tremendous moment that would have been. In the following forty days, why didn't He call a press conference? Think what TV could have done with all that.

But instead, He said to a weeping woman, "Mary." At Emmaus, He broke bread. On the side of the Sea of Galilee, He said, "Throw your net out on the other side of the boat, and you'll get some fish." What a strange way to start the greatest movement in all history.

There is a great danger today of us preachers trying to demonstrate the gospel the way this world demonstrates everything. It's true of all the Body of Christ. Having begun in the Spirit, we may try to perfect ourselves in the flesh.

When Paul came to Corinth from Athens, the center of worldly wisdom, his mind was made up to preach the foolishness of God, the gospel that the world calls moronic. That's where you get the word *moron*, from the word used in that passage. That made Paul a fool for Christ's sake, because if you are preaching a gospel that is to "the world foolishness," it automatically makes you, to the world, a fool.

We have practically forgotten that in a day when preachers are tempted to make themselves acceptable to the age instead of approved unto God. There has never been a culture since Christianity began in which a Christian could feel at home.

I think maybe one serious ailment is indicated in Psalm 119:54, where the psalmist said: "Thy statutes have been my songs in the house of my pilgrimage."

We're pilgrims and strangers and exiles and aliens. This is the house of our pilgrimage, and we have a song. We've been lifted out of the miry clay, our feet have been put on a rock, and a song has been put in our mouths. And what is that song? "Thy statutes."

What a strange term. Statutes made into songs? One never associates those two things. But God's law book is also a song book, and His mandates are also His melodies—words and music, theology and doxology.

Today, the danger is that in our vast religious establishment with its statistics and its wheels within wheels, its paraphernalia and its promotions, the mountain labors and brings forth a mouse.

I'm reminded of that maid who worked in a home where everything was elegant. The crystal and the silver were perfect, but they didn't have much to eat. She said, "The trouble here is there's too much shuffling of the dishes for the fewness of the victuals." I think we have discovered that today.

Ernest Hemingway said very truthfully, "We are deluged today with writers who can't write and actors who can't act and singers who can't sing, and they're all making a million dollars a year."

I remember years ago being in a service with a dear brother, sort of a whirling dervish, singing "Power in the Blood." He said, "Now we're going to have four powers in the next verse and then six powers in the next verse."

By the time we got around to six—POWer, POWer, POWer, POWer, POWer, POWer—I could have shut my eyes and thought I was listening to "Gunsmoke."

Even in the stiff, formal churches we've swung all the way from rigor mortis to St. Vitus.

We've got it right theologically, but there isn't a song. We've lost it. But, oh, it is always a great day when the church regains her song.

Think of the Wesleyan revival. Christianity was at a low ebb. The Puritans had all been buried, and the Methodists hadn't been born. That was a dark time. But the lowest ebb is the turn of the tide.

Then came John Wesley preaching and Charles Wesley singing the gospel: "Oh, for a thousand tongues to sing my great Redeemer's praise. My favorite verse is:

Hear Him, ye deaf; His praise, ye dumb,
Your loosened tongues employ;
Ye blind, behold your Saviour come;
And leap, ye lame, for joy.

When D. L. Moody went to Scotland, they had been having a church fuss. He set to music a tune that was haunting thousands of ears. Churchmen had been arguing the notes, but Moody and Sankey brought the music. The statutes became songs, and cold theology became warm doxology. What a difference! They found the lost radiance of the Christian faith, the joy of salvation that David lost, the first love that Ephesus left. Without it, it's art without heart and light without heat.

My preacher brother, if your sermon has no song, all that the listeners will get will be laryngeal sounds beating on eardrums. A Stradivarius in the hands of a master can lift you out of this world; but in the hands of a backwoods fiddler, all you hear is horsehair scraping on catgut. What makes the difference is the touch of the master's hand.

The greatest mission field in this world is the average Sunday morning congregation. Sardis had a name that it lived, but Sardis was play-acting. The more we seem to be what we are not, the smaller our chance of becoming what we ought to be. It takes a lot of hard work to keep up an illusion. Don't you ever think that it's easy to be a poser and to have a name that you're alive when you aren't.

Laodicea was a warm church, but don't forget that my Lord said, "I prefer a cold church to a warm church." Isn't it better to be a warm church than a cold church? No. The trouble with being lukewarm is that if you're cold, your very coldness may drive you to the fire.

But if you're just warm enough to be comfortable, you are insulated against any feeling of your need. We need to come to a boil today.

I'd like to testify to the fact that when I was thirty I had lost my song. I hadn't done anything terrible. There was no moral mark against me. But I'd lost my song. People began to ask whatever became of the boy preacher who started out at twelve.

One day, I came across a poem, and two little lines in it gripped me.

> How sad will be the days in store,
> When voice and vision come no more.*

That got me. World War I was over, and new thought was coming along. We had made the world safe for democracy.

*Author unknown.

Then came the Scopes trial with Clarence Darrow and William Jennings Bryan. The world applauded Darrow and ridiculed Bryan.

I went back to my old home in the hills. My father had died, a little disappointed that I wasn't turning out so well. He'd left a grocery store, and my mother and I sat there the winter through. Somebody robbed the store and burned it down.

God spoke to my soul and said, "If you'll get some of these new notions out of your head and go back and preach what you preached when you were a boy, I'll make a way for you." So I got out of the novelty shop and got back in the antique shop. God started opening the doors, and I've never lacked a place to preach from that day to this. He gave me a new message and a new mission.

Then God put me through a test. For two years I couldn't sleep at night, and I suffered from nervous exhaustion. I learned not to laugh at nervous people. I learned what it means. Then God called me to begin my preaching ministry. No doctor would have told me to go into this kind of work—sleeping in a different bed every week when I couldn't sleep in any bed.

And I said, "It doesn't make sense."

I finally said, "Lord, I'm going to make the venture, and if I'm wrong, stop me." That was a long time ago.

My first date was to be at Mel Trotter's mission in Grand Rapids, and I headed north in January. Any Southerner who heads for Grand Rapids in January is ailing a little bit. I got as far as Moody Bible Institute and came down with the flu. They put me in Augustana Hospital.

The devil sat on the foot of the bed and said, "Now what are you going to do? You've got no church, and you can't preach." But God remembered. He knew my frame and remembered that I was dust. I'd been invited to Florida Bible Institute and had turned them down. But now I wired them and said, "I'll come."

I went down there and met two remarkable people—a long,

lean, tow-headed student who came up to me and said, "I'm Billy Graham from Charlotte."

And then a little lady took pity on this poor, sick preacher. You know the way to a man's heart—she prepared soup and things that I could eat. She had faith enough to start out with a half-sick preacher who didn't have any money much and didn't know whether he could do this or not. She hadn't been so strong herself; but God was with us, and we never cracked up for thirty-three years.

I say this because, if you get to a place where you don't know what to do, give God the benefit of the doubt. He will clear the track.

Then after thirty-three years, God took her home, and I couldn't understand. I had to learn a still newer song. Sometimes your best song comes in your darkest hour: "When they had sung a hymn, they went out into the mount of Olives. And it was night." "At midnight Paul and Silas prayed and sang praises unto God." "He giveth songs in the night."

Sidlow Baxter was with me recently in a conference. He said his wife, who had been quite ill, had been healed. Well, God does heal, but not always. He didn't heal my Sarah. She died at 2:15 on a Sunday morning, and I preached at 11:00.

I didn't know whether I could, but I took for my text the question John the Baptist asked of my Lord, "Art thou he that should come, or do we look for another?" Jesus sent word back that He was running on schedule. The blind were seeing, the deaf hearing, the lame walking, and the lepers were being cleansed. Then He added what I call the forgotten beatitude: "Blessed is he, whosoever shall not be offended in Me." Blessed is the man who never gets upset by the way God runs His business.

I said, "Lord, I don't understand it. I thought we'd have a sweet old age together, and here I'm left like I started; but You know what You're doing."

I wrote a little book, and I have never in all these years had such a response to anything I've written. There's not a day that goes by that some dear soul in bereavement, sorrow, or trouble writes. I never had so many precious notes and letters from folks in Illinois and in Michigan, and Indiana, and Ohio.

You see, I'd had the statutes all the time. I believed them, but I didn't have the song. I'd lost it. But in that dark hour I found it. How this world does need compassion.

God has added a new dimension and a new note to my preaching. I have become a chaplain to the lonely and a comforter to the brokenhearted. I went out to a great church in Texas; and when I got there, the single adults were having a conference. They said, "Talk about loneliness, because that's our greatest problem."

We've never had more amusement and entertainment than we have today, but we've never had more lonely people. Last year set a record for suicide among teenagers. We're lonely.

But, my preacher friend, don't stomp on sinners when you go out to preach. My Lord didn't come to condemn the world, but that the world through Him might be saved. Bless God, He didn't come down here to rub it in; He came to rub it out. Tell them that.

And how do we get our song back? Second Chronicles 29:27: "When the burnt offering began, the song of the Lord began."

You won't have any song in your heart until the sacrifice is on the altar. The sacrifice of penitence—"The sacrifices of God are a broken spirit: a broken and a contrite heart, O God, thou wilt not despise" (Psalm 51:17). The sacrifice of person—"Present your bodies" (Romans 12:1). The sacrifice of praise—"The fruit of our lips giving thanks to his name" (Hebrews 13:15). That's the divine order.

Now a certain percentage of preachers and Christian workers have lost their song. It isn't that you don't believe what you've always believed. You're the last one to find it out. Your wife may know it, the church may know it, but you don't know it. Some resign, and some become resigned to such a state; but some seek God's face until they are "re-signed" with the stamp of God. Now, if you're playing the notes and not the music and if you have the statutes but not the song, don't go out and crack jokes over a steak tonight. Get alone and stay alone until God gives you a new song in the house of your pilgrimage.

We're facing a demonized world, and the only way to meet that *demon*-stration is with a demonstration of the Spirit of God and of power. The good news has been denied, it's been defended, and it's been declared; but what it needs most is to be demonstrated. The best argument for Christianity is a Christian.

There is nothing distinctive about many church members today. They've lost their identity because they've lost their identification. They're lost in the crowd, assimilated, amalgamated, homogenized, and meshed into the mass.

There's a time for the *declaration* of the gospel. Paul said, "I declare to you the gospel." There's a time for the *defense* of the gospel. Paul said, "I am set for the defense of the gospel." There's a time for the *demonstration* of the gospel. Paul said, "Christ liveth in me," and that's the best way to demonstrate it. The gospel works, but the world needs to see it work in you and in me.

If we're the light of the world, why is everything so dark? If we're the salt of the earth, why is everything so corrupt? There's something wrong with the demonstration. Too many candles are under the bushel or under the bed; too much Christian salt has lost its savor.

We need to get our eyes cleared up. You can't be optimistic with a misty optic. Get your eyes open, and when you do, you'll see that "there are more with us than they that be with them," as Elisha told his servant. I think also of that captain whose little band was completely surrounded by the enemy. His subordinate officer said, "Oh, they've got us this time. We're completely surrounded."

The captain said, "Good. Don't let one of them escape." That's the attitude we ought to take today.

As we older preachers get older, we're in great danger of

saying, "Well, I've had it. There remaineth no more land to be possessed. I'm going to coast on through to retirement." You're not looking for much to happen, and it won't.

I've had my three score ten and a bonus. I'm supposed to be sitting around in a rocking chair, drawing my social security, and reminiscing about the good old days that weren't so good. But I've got more open doors today than I've ever had in all these years.

One of my prayers is Psalm 71:18: "Now also when I am old and greyheaded, O God, forsake me not; until I have shewed thy strength unto this generation, and thy power to every one that is to come."

Some of you are not as young as you used to be. But you can have some snow on the roof and still have a fire in the furnace to the glory of God. Don't give up the battle. I'm having the time of my life. I don't know how I make it. I don't have any secretary, don't have an organization, don't have any foundation except the one that's laid by faith in His excellent Word. I don't run any magazine, any TV program, any radio outlets. You can still make it just preaching.

I watched Leopold Stokowski at ninety-four conduct a symphony and Rubenstein play the piano at ninety. We've got a preacher down in the mountains in North Carolina who is a hundred and five.

Oh, don't retire until God retires you, or I should say until He promotes you. His servants shall serve Him there. I've worked all the time down here, and I don't want to sit around on my cloud plucking a harp all through eternity. I want to do something.

Thank God there are all kinds of speeds—three speeds in the Christian life: "Mount up with wings as eagles"—that's high gear; "run and not be weary"—that's intermediate. Thank God you can "walk and not faint." There's grace for all gears, and even your youth can be renewed as the eagle's. You can have a rally in the last inning and still win the game. I'm on my way home, and I'm going to finish my course. I pray it may be with joy.

When I was growing up in the foothills of the Blue Ridge Mountains, no matter where I went in the afternoon it was understood that I was supposed to be back by sundown. We didn't discuss it, Father and I. We didn't do much dialoguing back in those days.

Well, it's been a long time since then, and I'm at the other end of the road now. I find myself praying, "Lord, I want to get home before dark, before I lose my faculties." I tell you, we can get in pitiful condition before we leave this world sometimes. I think of those precious lines that dear Dr. Culbertson liked, and this is just part of it, "Lord, when Thou seest that my work is done, let me not linger on with failing powers, a workless worker in a world of work." That's been my prayer.

I'd like to get home before dark because although you're saved, you're never safe as far as your testimony's concerned until you get home. They will all remember the big blunder you made on the last mile of the way and forget all the good things you did all the way back up the road.

Anthony Eden died, and what a magnificent man he was. What a great statesman. He had so much in his favor, but he, I suppose, made an error of judgment in that Suez affair, and everybody says, "Yes—but there was Suez."

When I started out as a boy preaching, Father went along. Then when I got old enough to go by myself, he'd meet me at the little railroad station in Newton, North Carolina. I can see him standing there by that old Ford roadster, in that old blue serge suit that hadn't been pressed since the day he bought it.

When I'd go up to him, the first thing he'd ask me would be, "How did you get along?"

It's been a long time, and one of these days when my train rounds into Grand Central Station in glory, I think he'll be there—not in the old blue serge suit, but in the robes of glory.

I wouldn't be surprised if the first thing he'd say would be, "How did you get along?"

I think I'll say, "Pretty well, and I owe a lot to you for it." Then I think I'd say, "You remember back in the country when I was a little boy, no matter where I was in the afternoon I was supposed to be back by sundown. It's been a long trip, Dad, but here I am by the grace of God, home before dark."

May that be the experience of every one of us.

## TWILIGHT ON THE TRAIL
## OF LIFE

Jesus is all we have; He is all we need and all we want. We are shipwrecked on God and stranded on omnipotence!

# Twilight on the Trail of Life

Survival is no longer the main issue with us senior citizens. Our life span has been lengthened, and machines keep us overtime. What matters most is the quality of life.

A ninety-year-old man was leaving on a trip around the world. An old friend lamented, "You ought not try a trip like this. I might not see you again."

The departing gentleman replied, "Maybe not. You may be dead when I get back!"

Birthdays tell us how long we have been on the road, but not how far we have traveled. God did not call me to preach only until I was sixty-five, then retire. He called me to preach, period. I'm preaching more than ever now with more open doors for my message than in years past. Retirement can be deadly.

How shall we oldsters best travel life's twilight trail? Longfellow put it well:

> What then? Shall we sit idly down and say,
> The night hath come, it is no longer day?
> The night hath not yet come, we are not quite
> Cut off from labor by the failing light:
> Something remains for us to do or dare,
> Even the oldest trees some fruit may bear.
> For Age is opportunity no less
> Than Youth itself though in another dress.
> And as the evening twilight fades away
> The sky is filled with stars invisible by day.

Age has forced no seriously radical changes on my life program. My habit of walking and meditating has paid off. A reservoir of reflections and a backlog of truth stand me in good

155

stead now. I am glad I remembered my Creator in horse-and-buggy days. I am alone now, without living wife or children. During the years since my companion went home to heaven, I have gained a new dimension and a new note. Passing through the Valley of Baca, I have managed to dig a few wells for other pilgrims (Psalm 84:6).

It helps to develop a sense of humor and common-sense thinking. For instance, I hear that word "terminal" so often nowadays. Actually, we all have a terminal ailment; we're all going to die. Everybody has to terminate, and some folks with a terminal disease may outlive hardier specimens.

The all-important thing is to know Jesus Christ as Savior, obey Him as Lord, and trust Him as our life. That life is eternal. It is ours now. There are many perplexing whys that have no answer at present. But we have not finished the book, and it is foolish to form conclusions before we get through. The grace of God gives us power for all three gears: to mount up as eagles, to run and not be weary, to walk and not faint.

The older generation has a vital place in the economy of God. We need youth to keep things from going too slowly and age to keep things from going too fast, although sometimes maturity and experience are sacrificed in favor of novices and novelties. But we senior citizens have better business than bemoaning the times and lamenting that things are not as good as they used to be. They never have been. Neither are we to keep silent in an evil time. The voice of experience is needed, and we had better speak before Rehoboam splits the kingdom.

Maintaining the spiritual "glow" when we have lost our "go" is a major problem. Sometimes I see smug older ministers who are coasting to retirement. It is next to impossible for a church to have a revival under such leadership, because the pastor himself needs reviving. Such Laodicean lukewarmness is not to be confused with that quietness and confidence that is our strength. An even-burning fire fueled by diligent use of the Word and prayer is better than an occasional burst of flame. That holds for any age.

Many aged people feel unwanted and unloved these days. Some may even have to adjust to an institution. This demands learning to be content in whatever state we are. Both youth and old age had better learn that getting through this world is no picnic. In it we shall have tribulation. But our Lord bade us be of good cheer, for He has overcome the world. We are not here to explain it or endure it or to enjoy it, but to overcome it. This is the victory that overcomes the world, even our faith. We shall make a go of it in any chapter from birth to death only as we share the life of Him who overcame.

Down here, things turn out in ways that simply don't add up in our little computers. There are no pat answers. The banes of our existence in such times are these dear cheer-up specialists who have never had much trouble themselves, who have convenient answers when they don't even know the question. We tolerate them and remind ourselves that Job's comforters are still among us.

Sometimes Romans 8:28 is not easy to accept. But Paul did not say, "We understand *how* all things work together for good" to the believer. He said, "We *know* that they do." We know many things we do not understand. One good look at Paul in his last days and, above all, at our Lord on Calvary, ought to silence our complaints. We are told that we are not tempted above what we are able to bear. This light affliction works for us a far more exceeding weight of glory.

If you draw near the end in somber circumstances, remember that as a faithful child of God you await promotion. Who knows but that the brightest jewel in your crown is for that lonely afternoon and night when all seemed lost but you believed anyway. Remember John the Baptist in prison and John on Patmos and countless millions who have been on that road before you. Remember Mr. Fearing in Bunyan's immortal *Pilgrim's Progress*, who dreaded Jordan all his days. But when he reached it, the water was at a record low, and he got across "not much above wet-shod."

The last chapter of life can be the best. Our greatest experience is not some spectacular trip to third heaven but when we learn that God's grace is sufficient. We learn this not in prosperity and success, but in the hour of desperate need. Old age can be such a time—when dearest loved ones have left us, when earthly resources are few, when body and mind begin to weaken. Then we learn to both sing and pray:

> Once earthly joy I craved,
> Sought peace and rest;
> Now Thee alone I seek,
> Give what is best.*

God becomes not only our Rewarder, but also our Reward. We find out that Jesus is all we have; He is all we need and all we want. We are shipwrecked on God and stranded on omnipotence. No price is too great to bring us that blessed experience. If we never learned it before, old age is a good time to discover it.

A few days ago I went up into the Virginia mountains looking for a remarkable old preacher. I had been on a vacation after a heavy schedule for many months. This old veteran was away preaching three weeks out of every month—and he is a hundred six! He thinks he'll be here when the Lord returns. I wanted to have a picture taken of us so that I could say for a change, "I'm the younger man." I came home and got to work.

All of us, young and old, ought to stop living as though this life were the end. It is not even the first chapter, only the preface. Now we see through a glass. In earlier times mirrors gave a warped and distorted image. Today our vision is blurred. But one day we'll see reality.

Paul had a rough time of it. He never stayed in a Riviera cottage writing his memoirs. He sat in a dingy Roman prison waiting to have his head chopped. But he had fought a good fight, finished his course, and kept the faith. He was waiting for a crown, anxious to depart and be with Christ, which is far, far better.

*Elizabeth P. Prentiss.

I find the last miles to be the best. When it's twilight on the trail, remember that the other side of sunset is sunrise. The other side of evening is morning; beyond death is life. One hour in heaven, and we shall be ashamed that we ever grumbled.

And who would go back and start over?

An old saint was asked, "Would you like to live your life again?"

"No," he answered, "I'm too near home!"